Eyewitness to Deceit

THE CANADIAN FEDERAL GOVERNMENT AND MAINSTREAM MEDIA CAMPAIGN OF DECEIT AGAINST FREEDOM CONVOY 2022

TOM QUIGGIN WITH RICK GILL

D1714279

QUOTES

*"They don't believe in science/progress and are very often misogynistic and racist. It's a very small group of people, but that doesn't shy away from the fact that they take up some space. This leads us, as a leader and as a country, to make a choice: **Do we tolerate these people**?"*

Prime Minister Justin Trudeau

"Whereas Canada is founded upon principles that recognize the supremacy of God and the rule of law:"

Preamble to the Canadian Charter of Rights and Freedoms

"It is dangerous to be right in matters on which the established authorities are wrong."

Voltaire - The Age of Louis XIV

"It's better to endure the discomfort of the truth now than to suffer the discomfort of the lie later."

Simon Sinek

DEDICATION

This book is dedicated to Corporal Thomas Hamilton, Private John Curwin, and Private Justin Jones of the Canadian Forces. They died in Afghanistan when their armoured vehicle was destroyed by an Improvised Explosive Device or IED.

The book is also dedicated to Corporal Chris Deering. He was the sole survivor of the attack that killed his three crewmates.

Chris Deering was awarded the Sacrifice Medal for his service in Afghanistan, following injuries sustained in the IED attack.

During Freedom Convoy 2022, he attempted to protect protestors who were engaged in a legal protest. He, along with other veterans, felt it was their role to protect protestors by placing themselves in harm's way between the police and protestors.

For his service to the country and his peaceful work with Freedom Convoy 2022, he was injured again; this time beaten to the ground by armed agents of the state under the direction of the Prime Minister.

Notwithstanding injuries sustained in both violent incidents, he remains dedicated to a peaceful path for a better Canadian future. He believes that the struggle for freedom in Canada may be the biggest battle of this generation.

CONTENTS

PREFACE

Corporal (retired) Danny Bulford, Royal Canadian Mounted Police

The government under Prime Minister Trudeau has consistently run a campaign of deceit against Freedom Convoy 2022 and any other individual or organization that opposes his views. This includes arrests and investigations that appear to be harassment and intimidation. My detention was based on an alleged media report that, apparently, never existed.

A History of Service

My family has a long history of service with the Royal Canadian Mounted Police. My father served 38 years in the Mounties. I have a brother who is a serving Mountie and another brother who has since left the force. My sister is a full-time career civilian member of the RCMP.

I joined the RCMP in August 2006 and left in December 2021. My decision to leave was based on the issue that I was speaking out against the way the RCMP had abandoned its core values. While serving in the RCMP, I was trained as a sniper and was part of the RCMP National Division Emergency Response Team (ERT) based in Ottawa, Ontario. During my time on the National Division ERT, my primary role was that of a sniper and observer, with most of my time spent supporting the protection of the Prime Minister and other internationally protected persons.

Freedom Convoy 2022

My role in Freedom Convoy 2022 was as a security coordinator and police liaison person. Most of my work time was spent at the Swiss Hotel operations centre. In that capacity, my responsibility was to recruit, schedule, and direct resources and personnel. This activity was based on incoming information and developing events. A continuous process of triage resulted in information being shared with police liaison officers.

A variety of individual situations also required attention. A series of threats were expressed against the doctors who spoke at convoy events. A particularly serious issue arose around an individual attempting to gain access to one doctor. The convoy also had to deal with surveillance being conducted against Tamara Lich from the rooftop of a building adjacent to her hotel. It remains unclear if the surveillance was carried out by a state organization, the media, or other individuals.

Social Media Influencers

As for Jeremy MacKenzie and Pat King, the public should be aware that neither of these individuals played any role in running convoy operations in Ottawa. To the best of my knowledge, they played no part in decision-making and never had access to such capabilities.

As such, the ongoing prosecutions of them by the Government of Canada should be seen in that context. The prosecutions are essentially persecutions aimed at intimidating those who speak out against government policies.

Jeremy MacKenzie was a social media activist who was active in Ottawa during the time of Freedom Convoy 2022. While you can choose to agree or disagree with his (Charter protected) free speech, he had no physical access to the decision-making areas and at no point was he involved in influencing outcomes. Still, the media and the Government of Canada are attempting to portray him as part of a 'militia.' The Government of Canada went so far as to suggest that 'Diagalon' was an extremist threat that was aiming to accelerate a racist war. Diagalon is a meme-producing satire operation based on a fictional territory created by the Raging Dissident podcast. For instance, the 'territory' of Diagalon has a vice emperor who is a goat figurine named Phillip who has a narcotic problem and likes to time travel. Still, several so-called experts, some of them paid by the Government of Canada, are trying to portray Jeremy/Diagalon as the face of the convoy which was also a threat to national security. It is a meme, not a threat.

Pat King also has/had a large social media following. The CBC, for instance, ran a Fifth Estate program on him and attempted to portray him as the face of the convoy. As recently as the 11th of June 2022, the CBC continued to portray him as a "Freedom Convoy leader."

The problem with the CBC (and others) is that Pat King had no access to the various decision-making processes. His self-described role was just that – self-described. He did have a loyal group of followers who paid close attention to his work. But as with Jeremy MacKenzie, he did not influence the day-to-day operations of Freedom Convoy 2022. Still, the media and the Government of Canada have attempted to portray him as a dangerous insurrectionist who played a leading role in the convoy.

In both cases, the media and the Government of Canada created a fiction to suit their own narratives.

Concerning the final police attack on the convoy, it strikes me that the highly aggressive tactics used to smash truck windows by the Emergency Response Team were questionable. Such tactics are only used in high-risk situations where firearms may be present. Was there any credible intelligence or information available to the police that weapons were present in trucks in Ottawa? Will we ever know what prompted the police to do this?[1]

The Narrative

My overall view of the response of the Government of Canada is that it was a complete fabrication. I make this assessment based on my real-world, firsthand experience of the convoy which was the opposite of the narratives created by the media in support of the government. It was an intentional effort to mislead Canadians and create further divisions by using hate-filled rhetoric and labeling groups/persons with derogatory terms. The entire effort can be characterized as a continuing series of vague statements presented with no evidence.

Comment by Author Tom Quiggin

For the record, both Danny Bulford and I would be willing to testify in civil or criminal court that Jeremy MacKenzie and Pat King played no managerial or directing role in Freedom Convoy 2022 from the 28th of January 2022 to the 20th of February 2022.

---

[1] Author's note: This situation is partially addressed in Chapter Eight "Loaded Shotguns."

INTRODUCTION

Almost from its inception, Canada's Freedom Convoy 2022 was subjected to a barrage of deceit by the Government of Canada. Canada's mainstream media followed suit and published articles filled with false or misleading information, rather than reporting the issues or events in an objective or unbiased manner. They claimed to have fears of violence and insurrection deriving from the Freedom Convoy.

This book is not a history or overall assessment of the Freedom Convoy 2022 movement from December 2021 to its dispersal in February 2022. The Freedom Movement that began with the convoy continues to grow in Canada and internationally. Documenting that is a larger project for a future date.

The purpose of this book is to unmask the Government of Canada and the mainstream media by detailing how they set out to destroy the Freedom Convoy with multiple deceitful narratives. Each major deceitful narrative created will be shown to be false. Like dominos, the narratives have fallen one by one as factual information has been revealed.

To understand why this was done, it is necessary to examine the larger ideologies and objectives at play in Ottawa at the time.

The narrow objectives of the Freedom Convoy 2022 were to push back against a series of vaccine mandates, especially those that governed cross-border travel and trade. The final action that created the Convoy was the seemingly arbitrary and capricious decision by the Government of Canada to impose severe vaccine mandate requirements on the trucking industry more than a year and a half into the pandemic.

The Freedom Convoy was never the 'anti-vaxxer' organization as was claimed by the federal government and the media. Most of the participants had been vaccinated and stated so publicly. The objective of the Freedom Convoy was not to address the vaccinations per se, but rather to protest the arbitrary application of 'mandates' and other rules that had no legal basis or foundation in Canadian law.

None of the organizers of the Convoy advocated for an overthrow of the Government of Canada. However, all sorts of individuals and organizations jumped on board, claiming they had a Convoy role where none existed. Many of those were hoping to enhance their profile or advance their agenda. This is, of course, a problem with a group of individuals that was a movement, rather than an organization.

Claims by the Government of Canada that this was a highly organized threat to democracy and the government were pure fantasy. Some of those making the claim may have done so out of pure ignorance, while others who knew better, did so out of malice. The Convoy can no more be blamed for what others outside their reach did any more than the Government of Canada can be blamed for its citizens committing crimes overseas.

The Ottawa City Council, the Province of Ontario, the Government of Canada, and a few academics repeatedly attempted to insinuate that the Convoy had malicious actors in it. Again, this is deceit. Freedom Convoy 2022 had a variety of individuals in support roles who had considerable real-world expertise in military, policing, counterterrorism, and paramedic operations.

A variety of mainstream media reporters expressed their fear or discontent with their treatment by Freedom Convoy participants. They would, for instance, complain they were not invited to press conferences. But, when the mainstream media was invited to the Freedom Convoy doctors' briefing on 11 February 2022, not even one was present. Perhaps they were afraid that their cherished narrative on the vaccine mandates would be challenged? Other members of the press would fabricate stories (e.g., that Putin was behind the convoy) and then complain that their credibility was openly challenged by Freedom Convoy 2022. The mainstream media, already suffering from low trust ratings well before the Convoy, dug the hole even deeper for itself.

Words Matter

The Government of Canada and the mainstream media used certain words in their attempt to discredit the actions of Freedom Convoy 2022. It was claimed that Ottawa was suffering under an 'occupation' and that the city was under 'siege.' Other stories suggested that the entire city had been blockaded. These were, of course, false. At any point during the Freedom Convoy protests, taxis and private cars were able to reach every street except Wellington Avenue itself. Even that had one lane open for police, fire, or paramedic services. Outside of the four blocks south of Wellington and parts of Sussex Avenue, all other streets and areas of Ottawa were open to the public.

Ultimately, it can be said that Freedom Convoy 2022 inadvertently shone a bright light on the deceit of the Canadian Government and much of the mainstream media. While the intent had been to protest the mandates, Freedom Convoy 2022 exposed the deceit of the Government of Canada and the dysfunction of government, at all three levels, when challenged by citizens' protests. Concurrently, Freedom Convoy 2022 exposed how much of the media twisted itself and its logic to support the government with willful misinformation campaigns.

The failure of the government and the media campaign of deceit to undercut Freedom Convoy 2022 led to the decision to impose the Emergency Measures Act. The government could not meet any of the four 'tests' required to do so but imposed this most draconian measure. By carrying out this action to punitively attack legal protestors while frightening anyone who supported it, the Government of Canada proved Voltaire to be correct.

"It is dangerous to be right in matters on which the established authorities are wrong."[2,3]

[2] François-Marie Arouet (Voltaire), "It Is Dangerous to Be Right in Matters Where Established Men Are Wrong." Quotepark.com, June 3, 2021, https://quotepark.com/quotes/1839239-voltaire-it-is-dangerous-to-be-right-in-matters-where-estab/.

[3] François-Marie Arouet (Voltaire), "Quotes from Work Le Siècle De Louis XIV (Voltaire)," Quotepark.com, accessed April 3, 2022, https://quotepark.com/works/le-siecle-de-louis-xiv-6902/.

CHAPTER 1: FREEDOM CONVOY 2022

The genesis of Freedom Convoy 2022 is to be found with the Canada Border Services Agency (CBSA) in Ontario.

Much of the public and government discourse around the convoy suggests that it was started and run from Alberta. As with many of the other accusations generated by the Government of Canada and the mainstream media, the reality does not match the narrative.

Freedom Convoy 2022 had multiple points of origin. The pandemic. The mandates. Canadians' fatigue with corruption and the politics of identity. Inflation. Decreasing lifestyles. Media capture by the Government of Canada. The loss of accountability in government.

But where and when was the moment where an individual said 'enough – I am going to do something.'

That moment was 16 November 2021 at the Windsor Bridge border crossing. A Canadian truck driver arrived at the border seeking to re-enter Canada after making a cargo run into the United States.

The driver, a Canadian citizen with strong roots and a long-term employment record in Ontario, became the victim of another example of strong-armed government overreach. A victim of domestic abuse in the past, the driver had discovered, to her surprise, that wearing a mask had triggered violent memories of suffocation in the past. As such, she had worn a visor at previous border crossings in compliance with pandemic restrictions. There had been no early problems with this in previous border crossings.

On this occasion, however, the armed CBSA guards insisted she wear a mask and threatened her with arrest if she did not immediately comply. Despite stating her situation and compliance, she was faced with two, and sometimes three, armed male border guards. The 5'2" female truck driver felt terrified. How can you be arrested for not wearing a mask when working in isolation? Furthermore, the event took place outdoors.

As a result of this incident, and multiple earlier incidents of facing harassment and overreach from armed Canadian government officials, she said "I'm done." The cumulative effects of almost two years' worth of COVID-19 restrictions plus financial losses and the threat of arrest, put her into a very dark place where she considered suicide.

A formal complaint to the CBSA was simply brushed off in a letter dated 31 December 2022.

Once released from the Windsor border crossing, the driver began to wonder if she was alone in her thinking about the abusive nature of the Canadian government and its overreach. It was especially concerning because, by this point, the pandemic was supposedly on its way down, but the government was discussing more abusive regulations aimed at truck drivers.

How was it possible, she asked, that truckers had been heralded as the saviours of the population by continuing to work throughout the pandemic, only to become targets of government abuse?

Following the 16 November incident, she posted a TikTok video with her views. She also began to search online forums to see what others were saying in response to the current events involving Covid, the mandates, and the Government of Canada.

To her surprise, many others were making similar postings and asking questions.

The Spark

It is a reach, of course, to say the CBSA caused Freedom Convoy 2022. It is fair, however, to say that they provided the spark that lit the fire.

On 28 June 1914, a Bosnian Serb Black Hand assassin killed the Austrian Archduke Ferdinand in Sarajevo. Most historians writing about World War One (The Great War) point to this moment as the key event that set Europe on the path to war. They are also clear that it was not just the assassination. Europe was suffering from aging empires, corrupt royal families, competition between nations for influence, and a naval arms race among many other problems.

The same can be said here. The CBSA border guards were probably not trying to cause Freedom Convoy 2022. Nonetheless, they played a formative role in the event, just as Gavrilo Princip[4] played his part in history.

Brigette Belton

Following the Windsor Bridge border crossing incident, truck driver Brigette Belton began reaching out to others through social media. Between them, they agreed that "something" had to be done. Following the Christmas holidays of 2021, a variety of conversations were occurring on social media. One suggestion was to have a convoy or group of convoys assemble for a protest in Ottawa against the mandate.

By 3 January 2022, conversations were advancing with discussions of various individuals organizing in their home areas. Slowing rolling the border was one initial idea that did not come to fruition at that point.

By 11 January 2022, the first poster was created advocating a "Convoy to End the Mandates." The poster stated that:

> *"WE ARE ALL IN THIS TOGETHER IN OUR FIGHT FOR FREEDOM - VACCINATED OR UNVACCINATED. JOIN OUR CONVOY. 23 JANUARY WE SLOW ROLL EVERY PROVINCE UNTIL THE MANDATES STOP"*

The now (in)famous GoFundMe campaign only started on 14 January 2022. Its organizer, Tamara Lich, had been contacted by the other organizers and asked if she could take on this role. So, despite the media focus (blame?) on her for her role as 'leader,' the reality is somewhat different.

---

[4] Editors, "Gavrilo Princip," Encyclopædia Britannica, April 24, 2022, https://www.britannica.com/biography/Gavrilo-Princip. **Rated B1.**

From early January 2022 onwards, many others besides Brigette began to play organizing and supporting roles. Many of their names are well known, and others are not so well known. The larger history of the convoy is yet to be written, a project that will require many authors.

Lack of Arrest

Questions have been raised as to who was arrested and who was not. Brigette believed at several points that she might be arrested given her formative, if low-profile, role. Others were arrested such as Tamara Lich and Chris Barber.

Brigette believes that her previous employment with the City of Ottawa (ten years) may have played a role. She had also worked for City Councillor and Ottawa Police Board member Eli El-Chantiry[5] in a private industry role and was familiar with a variety of police and civic officials in Ottawa. As such, she may have been an awkward target due to her Ottawa and Ontario connections when the government and media narrative was that it was an Alberta problem.

It is also possible to probable that Tamara Lich was jailed and held without bail due more to her profile rather than her actual role. As a Metis woman, it can also be said that she presents an easy target, especially

---

[5] City of Ottawa, "Eli El-Chantiry - Councillor - Ward 5 West Carleton-March," City of Ottawa, March 10, 2021, https://ottawa.ca/en/city-hall/mayor-and-city-councillors/eli-el-chantiry. **Rated B1.**

given the role of Prime Minister Trudeau in abusing native women (think Jody Wilson-Raybould[6]).

The police in general relied on media reporting for many of their actions rather than any internal assessment or intelligence. Danny Bulford, a former RCMP sniper, was arrested and held for several hours, based on the police reading a media report that an arrest warrant had been issued for him. No arrest warrant had ever been issued, so he was falsely arrested and held in jail on a media report. Such was the nature of events surrounding Freedom Convoy 2022.

Assessment

Despite a media and government narrative that the Freedom Convoy was created in Alberta, the reality is that the genesis of the convoy was in Ontario and Windsor in particular.

The CBSA provided the spark that lit the fire. The problem, as many believe, is the Government of Canada's arbitrary and unconstitutional ending of individual rights and freedoms while providing no scientific evidence for their decisions. This in turn has created a political space where minor functionaries feel entitled to carry out abusive actions which many of them must know are leading us down a dangerous path.

---

[6] Editors, "The Honourable Jody Wilson-Raybould," Members of Parliament - House of Commons of Canada (Government of Canada, September 19, 2021), https://www.ourcommons.ca/members/en/jody-wilson-raybould(89494)/roles. **Rated B1.**

Freedom Convoy 2022 was also attacked in its formative stages for being an "anti-vaxxer" organization. This is false. From its inception to the police attacks following the implementation of the Emergencies Act, the convoy was pro-choice rather than anti-vax. Most of its leadership was double vaccinated. The poster of 11 January shows this idea was built into the DNA of the movement.

Separate from Freedom Convoy 2022 itself, it is worth noting that the time from the initial spark of 16 November 2021 to the arrival of the Freedom Convoy in Ottawa was essentially two months. Seen through a narrower lens, the organizational time in question is one month. This is based on an analysis of online discussions from late December to the arrival of the convoy in late January.

By the time of its arrival in late January, the Freedom Convoy had already sparked a nationwide wave of support that reached from the far north to British Columbia and to Newfoundland. The rapidity of its growth, despite a government and media slur campaign against it, highlight the degree to which discontent was underlining Canadian society at the time.

Following the arrival of Freedom Convoy 2022 in Ottawa, the movement took on an international dimension. Again, this goes to show that many persons, especially the lower and middle class believe they have been left out of government and that they do not matter.

The process of "elite capture" with its destructive nature on democracy, freedom of speech, and societal stability has been identified as an issue. Freedom Convoy 2022 identified the issues and did not create them. How this plays out is yet to be seen.

CHAPTER 2: ASSESSING INFORMATION

Governments often use false information to advance their policies or strategies. This is a difficult problem in a time of civil unrest or war. The expression "In war, truth is the first casualty" is attributed to the Greek playwright Aeschylus writing around 550 B.C.

Such was the case with Freedom Convoy 2022. The Government of Canada began a disinformation (propaganda) campaign at the outset. This became increasingly evident as time progressed. This book will show that a variety of false narratives and accusations were advanced by the Government of Canada and supported by compliant media.

It is a reasonable question to ask, however, about who gets to be the arbiter of information. Who decides if it is true or not?

The approach used in this book will be to provide a variety of examples of the narratives put forth by the Government of Canada and the mainstream media. This will show the public statements they were making.

Following that, evidence will be produced to show that the statements were false or misleading. In many cases, the evidence will also show the Government and media continued to make the same false statements even after the statements were shown to be false by the proper and relevant authorities.

Standards of evidence vary. In the case of this book, the standard of evidence used will be that of what is acceptable in the Federal Court of Canada which hears civil cases. This will be the 'balance of probabilities' which is the standard of proof for a civil case, in contrast to that for a criminal case which is proof beyond a reasonable doubt.[7]

In addition to the Federal Court standard of evidence, this book will also assess most individual information sources using the Revised Admiralty Rating System (See Annex A). This system was created by the Royal Navy in World War Two to systematically evaluate, and rate mass volumes of reporting being received from a wide variety of sources.

The system has many advantages. Perhaps most importantly, it forces the analyst to develop a mental framework where they assess not just one, but rather the two relevant factors: *Source Reliability and Information Credibility.* In many cases, including the courtroom, information analysis fails as the analyst (or lawyer) accepts the idea that the source is 'reliable.' The failure occurs when a second assessment does not occur: Is the information credible? All too often, a source who is reliable may still provide information that is incorrect or misleading. This may not be malice, but rather competency or capability.

The Admiralty System, therefore, provides a two-part scale of assessment. The first is an A to F rating on source reliability which shows if the source over time has been completely reliable down to unreliable or cannot be judged. It then assigns a 1 to 6 rating for the credibility of the information. These ratings range from

---

[7] Department of Justice, "Civil and Criminal Cases," About Canada's System of Justice (Government of Canada, September 1, 2021), https://justice.gc.ca/eng/csj-sjc/just/08.html. **Not Rated.**

'no doubt' of credibility down to 'willfully deceptive' or unable to judge.

For example, a report or information received from a source that is "usually reliable" and whose information provided at that point in time is believed to be "probably true" would be rated as "B2". A **"Rated C4"** assessment would indicate a source is fairly reliable; however, this information is doubtful. A **"Rated F6"** assessment would indicate that source reliability and information credibility cannot be judged.

Personal Background

Over the last thirty-five years, I have worked in a variety of intelligence roles. These have included the Canadian Armed Forces[8], UNPROFOR[9], the Privy Council Office of Canada[10], the Royal Canadian Mounted Police,[11] Citizenship and Immigration Canada[12] as well as Nanyang Technological University in Singapore.[13] Each

---

[8] Editors, "Intelligence Officer," Intelligence Officer | Canadian Armed Forces (Department of National Defence, 2022), https://forces.ca/en/career/intelligence-officer/. **Not Rated.**

[9] Editors, "United Nations Protection Force (UNPROFOR) Former Yugoslavia," United Nations, August 31, 1996, https://peacekeeping.un.org/mission/past/unprof_p.htm.

[10] Editors, "Privy Council Office (PCO)," Canada.ca (Government of Canada, May 11, 2022), https://www.canada.ca/en/privy-council.html.

[11] Editors, "Royal Canadian Mounted Police," Royal Canadian Mounted Police (Government of Canada, May 17, 2022), https://www.rcmp-grc.gc.ca/.

[12] Editors, "Immigration, Refugees and Citizenship Canada," Canada.ca (Government of Canada, March 27, 2018), https://www.canada.ca/en/immigration-refugees-citizenship/corporate/mandate.html.

of these positions has involved an ongoing need to assess information and intelligence. I was also the security and operational risk manager for the Bank of Canada.[14]

I have testified in multiple court cases in both criminal and civil courts. Additionally, I have testified to the Senate of Canada, the House of Commons of Canada, and the Air India Royal Commission of Inquiry.

Major Court Appearances and Testimony

- R. v. Ribich (Bosnian war hostage-taking) 2002
- R. v Momin Khawaja (Terrorism case bail hearing) - May 2004
- R. v Momin Khawaja (Terrorism case review, Ontario Superior Court) June 2005
- National Security Certificate Case Docket DES 3-08, Ottawa, October 2009,
- National Security Certificate Case, (Almrei) Toronto, May 2009
- Other testimony or evidence preparation includes less significant cases in the Immigration and Refugee Board court[15] process.

Court Expert

---

[13] Editors, "S. Rajaratnam School of International Studies (RSIS)," Think Tank and Graduate School (Nanyang Technological University, 2022), https://www.rsis.edu.sg/.
[14] Editors, "Risk Management," Bank of Canada, 2022, https://www.bankofcanada.ca/about/governance-documents/risk-management/.
[15] Editors, "Immigration and Refugee Board of Canada," Canada.ca (Government of Canada, April 13, 2022), https://www.canada.ca/en/immigration-refugee.html.

In a variety of court appearances, the judges involved have recognized my presence as a court expert or one who can give opinion testimony. These have included the following:

- Qualified as a court expert[16] by Mr. Justice Mosley of the Canadian Federal Court on 09 October 2008. The specific area of expertise was stated as: "Structure, organization, and evolution of the global jihadi movement." Federal Court Decisions, 2009-01-02, Citation 2009 FC 3, File number DES-3-08.

- Qualified as a court expert by Mr. Justice Roydon Kealey of the Ontario Superior Court on 07 June 2005. The case in question was R v Khawaja where the accused was charged with participating in the activity of a terrorist group and facilitating terrorist activity under s. 83.18 and 83.19 of the Criminal Code. The specific area of expertise was stated as: "Structure, organization, and evolution of the global jihadi movement." The Department of Justice file number is 1-377960 and the court information number is 04-30282.

- Qualified as a court expert on *"intelligence collection and reliability"* by the Federal Court of Canada in a decision released on 14

---

[16] Expert testimony, or opinion evidence as it is also called, may be given by a witness "who is shown to have acquired special or peculiar knowledge through study or experience in respect of the matters on which he or she undertakes to testify"

December 2009, Citation 2009 FC 1263, File number DES 3-08.[17]

Department of Justice Training

In addition to court testimony, I have also trained Special Advocate lawyers and judges[18] on the reliability of intelligence as evidence in a courtroom. They were as follows:

- July 7th, 2008 – Training for the Department of Justice Special Advocates Course on intelligence and evidence.
- May 26th, 2008 – Training for the Department of Justice Special Advocates Course on intelligence and evidence.

Assessment

The material provided as evidence in this book has been examined and rated. It is of sufficient strength that I believe it would withstand cross-examination in the Federal Court of Canada or a similar forum.

---

[17] The Honourable Mr. Justice Mosley, "Almrei (Re) 2009 FC 1263," Almrei (re) - Federal Court (Government of Canada, December 14, 2009), https://decisions.fct-cf.gc.ca/fc-cf/decisions/en/item/57473/index.do. **Not Rated.**
[18] Editors, "Special Advocates Program," Department of Justice (Government of Canada, August 20, 2021), https://www.justice.gc.ca/eng/fund-fina/jsp-sjp/sa-es.html.

CHAPTER 3: MY ROLE

My involvement with the Freedom Convoy 2022 began, by accident, on Tuesday, the 18th of January 2022. This was approximately three weeks after the main organization efforts for the Freedom Convoy had begun.

In the spring of 2019, I met Tamara Lich while on a speaking tour of Alberta. She had been one of the organizers of an event in Medicine Hat. The event had stood out for its detailed preparations. When I asked who had made the arrangements, I was introduced to her.

We had communicated five times by text in 2021 and had not communicated at all from September 2021 until the 18th of January 2022. On that day, I noticed that the federal Minister for the Environment had stated that Canada would be moving away from fossil fuels in 18 months.[19] I texted her to see how this view was playing out in Alberta.

The response from Tamara confused me. Her reply was "I'm just heading into a meeting with an accountant and bookkeepers. I was expecting a few thousand in donations and I just had to increase it to $400,000!"[20]

I had no idea what this was about.

Based on that response, I did an internet search to see what donations she was talking about. It took only a short time to find the GoFundMe website that had her

---

[19] Phone text of 18 January 2022 at 1:42 PM Eastern. **Rated A1**

[20] Phone text of 18 January 2022 at 1:53 PM Eastern. **Rated A1**

name on it. That was the first time I was made aware of Freedom Convoy 2022.

My involvement over the next 10 days was relatively minimal, confined mostly to providing contact names and numbers of persons in the media who might be interested in writing stories about the Freedom Convoy.

It is difficult to say exactly when, but by the 21st or 22nd of January 2022, I realized that the Freedom Convoy 2022 would be significantly different that the carbon tax convoy of 2018. The two "indications and warnings"[21] that were obvious to any observer were the rapidly increasing donations on the GoFundMe website and the large number of persons showing support for the Freedom Convoy. This could be seen by individuals cheering them on at roadside events or standing on overpasses as the convoy(s) passed. Much of this activity, of course, was occurring with the weather at minus 20 Celsius or worse.

More to the point, my previous experience with the Royal Canadian Mounted Police (2000-2006) told me this protest would be a more impactful event than earlier protests. This protest was likely to have a larger impact than previous protests such as those related to the G7/G8; a US presidential visit or the pro/anti-abortion protests.

Multiple reasons were evident for this belief:

- Broad support across Canada in multiple regions including Alberta and Quebec;

---

[21] "Indicators and Warnings" is a structured analytic technique used by intelligence analysts to see potential trends, indications, or warnings about future events.

- Physical turnout of supporters at events;

- Large numbers of small donations to the GoFundMe campaign;

- The rapid development of the Freedom Convoy from nothing to a national level;

- The early mainstream media attacks and their negative biases suggested real popular support;

- Verbal attacks from alt-left or progressive social media sites

- Attacks from so-called "anti-hate" sites which are pro-alt left efforts

Historically, major protests in Ottawa have featured several themes. Among them are anti-capitalist, anti-fiat currency, pro/anti-globalist ideology, pro/anti-open borders, pro/anti-abortion, pro-Palestinian/Hezbollah, and pro-anarchist themes. The largest of the protests resulted in a multiplicity of ideas and groups being represented – many of them in conflict with each other.

Several organizations were 'frequent flyers' at a variety of Ottawa-based protests. Among them were CLAC (Convergence des Luttes Anticapitalists or Anti-Capitalist Convergence) and No One Is Illegal. Other groups and individuals would also appear and support a wide range of ideologies and beliefs.

One feature of the protests in which I was involved was that most of the protestors were legitimate in the sense they did not advocate or practice violence. However, almost every protest attracted a fringe element of groups and individuals who specifically acted out with the intent of creating violence during the protests. They would speak in terms of "creating a physical space for alternative tactics" or they would speak of functioning in "the sacred space of the riot."

These groups largely self-identified as anarchists or anti-fascist in orientation and would openly speak of using 'black bloc' tactics. They would locate themselves on the fringes of the protests and attempt to provoke violent reactions using projectiles or physical provocation with other individuals. The intent was to create a violent police response which they then hoped would turn into a general riot. These individuals and groups were usually identifiable by their black jeans, black boots, black hoodies, and black masks. A few of those who advocated or practiced violence were from the Ottawa area, but a general pattern was observed whereby some of the worst elements would arrive from Montreal or the Greater Toronto Area.

Freedom Convoy 2022

Towards the end of January 2022, I decided to become involved in supporting the Freedom Convoy. Having worked extensively on Ottawa-based, large-scale protests, I believed that a limited number of outsiders, with no links to the Freedom Convoy, would use the event to provoke violence to further their agendas. Given my background in intelligence analysis for military, police, and civil authorities, I intended to create a series of intelligence-style reports on matters related to the Freedom Convoy. They would take the form of daily reports and the occasional special report on specific issues. These reports were posted on social media so that anyone with internet access could read them.

The nature of these reports was protective intelligence or what the military would call "force protection" when deployed to a conflict area such as the Former Yugoslavia[22] or Afghanistan. As I explained in a press conference, the intended function of my largely self-described role was to assess information, process it, and provide reports which would assist in protecting (in order):

- Truckers in the Freedom Convoy
- The police, fire, and paramedics on scene, and
- The general Ottawa population.

The first daily report was published on 27 January 2022 and the first special report was published on 28 January 2022.

The subject of the first special report was violence. One of the key points of that report was that the Government of Canada would:

"Create an atmosphere or a 'political space' whereby those who advocate violence as a distraction will find the opportunity to express it. This violence will express itself from extreme left forces such as Anti-Fa, a variety of political/religious extremist groups or small groups of those who would self-identify as anarchists, anarcho-syndicalists or anarcho-environmentalists."

As it turns out, this warning would prove to be accurate. The intrusion at the Shepherds of Good Hope Mission, for example, was not carried out by Freedom Convoy affiliates. The Ottawa arson attempt did not come from

---

[22] My role in the former Yugoslavia was an intelligence analyst at the UNPROFOR HQ. This included force protection, targeting, source analysis and other duties.

the Freedom Convoy affiliates. There were no attacks against any Members of Parliament, City Councillors, or police officers.

For the first two weeks after the Freedom Convoy's arrival, I attended a select number of events as well as participated in meetings. These meetings were an attempt to bring some sort of structure and order to the Freedom Convoy movement. Additionally, I photocopied and handed out copies of the Daily Report to police and paramedics on scene, as well as taking multiple walks through the protest areas.

By the 12th or 13 of February 2022, it had become clear to me that the Freedom Convoy movement was suffering internally. In addition to the money problems with GoFundMe, the organizational problems were worsening rather than improving. A variety of problems existed, primarily driven by a lack of internal communications, and competing agendas. The most debilitating problem, however, was that several late-arriving individuals were either deliberately or inadvertently creating rifts within the movement. This was a particular problem with those who had their private agenda or were using the convoy for their purposes.

From an intelligence point of view, it was proving difficult to be effective without being able to interact with an individual or group that was functioning in a leadership role. Most of my earlier work had been within highly structured environments. Even within the often-chaotic environment of the United Nations headquarters in Zagreb, Croatia, a relatively effective chain of command provided the necessary elements for a functioning force protection, source development, and targeting intelligence section.

N.B.: It remains a mystery to me how CSIS and the RCMP failed to warn the Government of Canada on the size, duration, and depth of support for the convoy. While both agencies have suffered from politicization and an unwillingness to be bearers of bad news, an intelligence failure of this magnitude is still difficult to grasp. Understanding that failure is a project for another time.

CHAPTER 4: A SAFE LOCATION

As the Freedom Convoy 2022 began to arrive in Ottawa on 28/29 January 2022, the Prime Minister of Canada fled the city. Among the first to report his departure was the state-funded CBC.

At 4:00 AM ET on the 29th of January 2022, the CBC ran a headline story that read: *Thousands opposed to COVID-19 rules converge on Parliament Hill.*

The key bit of information, however, was in the first line of the report after the title: It read:

> *Trudeau and his family have been moved from residence over security concerns.*[23]

The story stated that the Prime Minister and his family had been moved from their home to an undisclosed location somewhere within the National Capital Region. There was no identification of how the CBC knew that as the article stated the information was according to "sources." The Prime Minister's Office (PMO) said it could not comment on the whereabouts of Trudeau. His public itinerary normally gives his location for any given day, but for this date is stated only that he was in the National Capital Region.

---

[23] John Paul Tasker, "Thousands Opposed to COVID-19 Rules Converge on Parliament Hill | CBC News," CBC News Politics (CBC/Radio Canada, January 29, 2022), https://www.cbc.ca/news/politics/truck-convoy-protest-some-key-players-1.6332312. **Rated C4.**

27

The story was widely covered in both the domestic and international media as well as social media. Among the headlines were:

- *Justin Trudeau Flees to Secret Location.*[24]
- *Justin Trudeau was moved to a secret location as thousands in Canada protest COVID-19 vaccine mandates for truckers and other restrictions.*[25]
- *Justin Trudeau moved to secret location during Canada vax protests: report.*[26]
- *Justin Trudeau and family move to secret location as Canada trucker protests spark security fears, report says.*[27]

---

[24] Robert J. Lee, ed., "Justin Trudeau Flees to Secret Location," Cairns News, January 31, 2022, https://cairnsnews.org/2022/01/31/justin-trudeau-flees-to-secret-location/. **Rated C3.**

[25] Kelsey Vlamis, "Justin Trudeau Was Moved to a Secret Location as Thousands in Canada Protest COVID-19 Vaccine Mandates for Truckers and Other Restrictions," Yahoo! News (Yahoo!, January 29, 2022), https://news.yahoo.com/justin-trudeau-moved-secret-location-014736503.html. **Rated C3.**

[26] Emily Crane, "Justin Trudeau Moved to Secret Location during Canada Vax Protests: Report," New York Post (NYP Holdings, Inc., January 30, 2022), https://nypost.com/2022/01/30/justin-trudeau-moved-to-secret-location-during-vax-protests/. **Rated C3.**

[27] Josh Marcus, "Trudeau Moved to Secret Location as Canada Protests Spark Security Fears, Report Says," The Independent (Independent Digital News and Media, January 31, 2022), https://www.independent.co.uk/news/world/americas/justin-trudeau-trucker-convoy-protest-canada-b2003458.html. **Rated C3.**

- *'Tyrant On The Run': Internet Blasts Trudeau For Fleeing Capital As 'Freedom Convoy' Protest Heads His Way.*[28]

Before the arrival of Freedom Convoy 2022, Prime Minister Trudeau had already disappeared from public view – more than he had previously during the pandemic. The official reason given was that he was self-isolating for five days after having been exposed to COVID-19 on 26 January 2022.[29] He stated that he had tested negative but would isolate anyway.[30] This despite reports he had been triple-vaccinated.

After those five days of isolation, Prime Minister Trudeau was absent from the public view for at least another seven days. All told, he was in hiding for at least twelve days.[31]

---

[28] Amanda Prestigiacomo, "'Tyrant on the Run': Internet Blasts Trudeau for Fleeing Capital as 'Freedom Convoy' Protest Heads His Way," The Daily Wire, January 30, 2022, https://www.dailywire.com/news/tyrant-on-the-run-internet-blasts-trudeau-for-fleeing-capital-as-freedom-convoy-protest-heads-his-way. **Rated C3.**

[29] Editors, "Trudeau Says He's Isolating after Exposure to COVID-19," CBC News Politics (CBC/Radio Canada, January 27, 2022), https://www.cbc.ca/news/politics/trudeau-isolation-covid-1.6329476. **Rated C4.**

[30] Justin Trudeau, "Last Night, I Learned That I Have Been Exposed to Covid-19. My Rapid Test Result Was Negative. I Am Following @OttawaHealth Rules and Isolating for Five Days. I Feel Fine and Will Be Working from Home. Stay Safe, Everyone – and Please Get Vaccinated.," Twitter (Twitter Inc., January 27, 2022), https://twitter.com/JustinTrudeau/status/1486704226449379329. **Not Rated.**

The question of a sitting Prime Minister going into hiding from a peaceful protest drew considerable attention. Many suggested the problem was that he was a coward and chose to flee rather than confront the opposition.

One of those leading the discussion was public intellectual Dr. Jordan Peterson.[32] Dr. Peterson raised the question in a YouTube video[33] on 6 February 2022. The video was viewed 2,324,017 times as of this writing. The interview was carried out by #PBDPodcast. The title of the video was:

Is Justin Trudeau A Coward for Fleeing Canada During Freedom Convoy Protests?

Dr. Peterson describes the actions of Prime Minister Trudeau as one who "ran away" from a protest citing security concerns. He believes that Trudeau's departure was an instigation, given that there was no

---

[31] Harrison Faulkner, "Recap of Day 12 of Truckers for Freedom Convoy across Canada," True North (True North Centre for Public Policy, February 3, 2022), https://tnc.news/2022/02/03/recap-of-day-12-of-truckers-for-freedom-convoy-across-canada%ef%bf%bc/. **Rated B3.**

[32] Dr Jordan B. Peterson, "Is Justin Trudeau a Coward for Fleeing Canada during Freedom Convoy PROT... https://youtu.be/bZB36C5BGsk or https://twitter.com/jordanbpeterson/status/1490379072630894597. **Not Rated.**

[33] Patrick Bet-David, "Is Justin Trudeau A Coward For Fleeing Canada During Freedom Convoy Protests?," YouTube (Google LLC, February 6, 2022), https://www.youtube.com/watch?v=bZB36C5BGsk. **Not Rated.**

real security threat to the Prime Minister at that time. The protest had been entirely peaceful. Peterson feels that the message from Trudeau was "you people are dangerous and not to be trusted."

Dr. Peterson warned that the situation was developing in such as way that Prime Minister Trudeau had a proclivity to instigate further problems and it would be extraordinarily convenient for Mr. Trudeau. He added that this proclivity for instigation would be an easy out for the Prime Minister.

Assessment

My awareness of the Freedom Convoy began on the 18th of January 2022. Prime Minister Trudeau announced he was going into isolation on the 26th of January and that he was fleeing the capital for security reasons on the 29th of January.

By that time, my own experience in such matters had brought me to two private beliefs. First, he would never meet with the Freedom Convoy for the simple reason that he could not. The Government of Canada did not have any science-based information for their crackdown on truck drivers some 18 months into the pandemic.

My second belief was that Prime Minister Trudeau (advisor Gerald Butts?) was intent on creating a fake hysteria around the Freedom Convoy to discredit it and refuse to deal with it. This would be broadly consistent with their habit of calling anyone who disagreed with them alt-right Nazis[34] or racists.[35]

It is worth noting that Dr. Jordan Petersen also had a similar view that he expressed on the 6th of February 2022. In his mind, the incident of Trudeau fleeing the capital was an "instigation."

Foreshadowing from United We Roll 2019

It should be remembered that after the 2019 Carbon Tax convoy (United We Roll), the Privy Council Office (PCO) of the Government of Canada had worried about the outcomes.

According to PCO emails, "Many participants have voiced frustration with the PM personally, not only the federal government, with many calls for 'overthrowing' or arresting the PM."

According to the Clerk of the Privy Council (most senior bureaucrat in Canada) "I worry about the rising tide of incitements to violence when people use terms like treason and traitor in open discourse. Those are the words that lead to assassination. I'm worried that

---

[34] Gerald Butts, "The Lesson to Take from This Joke Being Torqued by Infowars and Other Alt-Right Nazi Friends of the Rebel Is They're Paying Attention. Game on, #TeamTrudeau," Twitter (Twitter Inc., February 8, 2018), https://twitter.com/gmbutts/status/961573323112112129. Gerald Butts is a long-time confident and senior advisor to Justin Trudeau. **Not Rated.**
[35] Unknown, "Trudeau Calls Quebec Woman Racist for Questioning Illegal Immigration," YouTube (Google LLC, August 19, 2018), https://www.youtube.com/?gl=DE. **Not Rated.**

somebody's going to be shot in this country this year during the political campaign." [36,37,38]

Of note, former Clerk of the Privy Council Michael Wernick made the above statement in a February 21st 2019 hearing at the Commons justice committee. Mr. Wernick presented these personal "worries" in an *evidence-free* manner as they were entered into the public record.

These sorts of *evidence-free* comments about possible violence in the 2019 convoy foreshadow the response of the PCO and PMO to the 2022 convoy. In both cases, there was never any evidence of an attempt to assassinate anyone, arrest the Prime Minister or storm the Parliament Buildings.

Interestingly enough, and relevant to Freedom Convoy 2022, PCO staffers also anticipated possible violence between United We Roll demonstrators and "people

---

[36] Zi-Ann Lum and Canadian Press, "Top Civil Servant Cautions Politicians of Using 'Words That Lead to Assassination'," HuffPost (The Huffington Post, February 21, 2019), https://www.huffpost.com/archive/ca/entry/michael-wernick-canada-election-violence-assassination_a_23675412. **Rated C1.**
[37] National Post, "Michael Wernick Speaks to Justice Committee," YouTube (Google LLC, February 21, 2019), https://www.youtube.com/watch?v=tXoffOVdd8U. **Rated C1.**
[38] Editors, "Evidence - Just (42-1) - No. 132 - House of Commons of Canada," Standing Committee on Justice and Human Rights meeting - House of Commons of Canada (Government of Canada, February 21, 2019), https://www.ourcommons.ca/DocumentViewer/en/42-1/just/meeting-132/evidence. **Rated B1.**

who are sympathetic to environmentalist, anti-colonialist and anti-fascist movements". This sort of associated violence occurred when individuals posing as convoy members attacked a homeless shelter in 2022.

CHAPTER 5: CBC AND THE RUSSIANS

Evidence-Free Broadcasting

The state-funded Canadian Broadcasting Corporation (CBC) deliberately produced false information on Freedom Convoy 2022 from the outset of its reporting.

On Friday, the 28th of January 2022, the Freedom Convoy began arriving in Ottawa, the CBC interviewed Public Safety Minister Mendocino. In that interview, Nil Köksald ran a deliberate and *evidence-free* smear on the Freedom Convoy. This smear piece would set the tone for much of the reporting that followed from the CBC and other government-subsidized media organizations. It should be noted that this interview occurred before the Russian invasion of Ukraine.

Nil Köksald questioned Minister Mendocino on the origins and support for the Freedom Convoy. See asked:

> *"I do ask that because given Canada's support of Ukraine, in this current crisis with Russia, I don't know if it's far fetched to ask but there is concern that Russian actors could be continuing to fuel things, as this protest grows, but perhaps even instigating it from the outset."*[39]

Ms. Köksald provided absolutely no evidence of any such Russian support. She did not quote other sources

---

[39] Editors, "Public Safety Minister Discusses Security Concerns around Protest Convoy," CBC News (YouTube, January 28, 2022), https://www.youtube.com/watch?v=MLKcfi9WLXA. **Rated C4.**

that might have made a similar claim. As it would be stated the next day by True North News:

> "CBC anchor invents conspiracy about Russia orchestrating freedom convoy."[40]

It is noteworthy that the Minister of Public Safety did not attempt to refute the premise of the question or challenge the false information. He responded by saying:

> "Well again, I'm going to defer to our partners at Public Safety, the trained officials and experts in that area."

It is worth noting that the fake allegations made by the CBC were not presented on a local channel or a minor news program. They were made on the program that the CBC states "is the arena where decision-makers answer the questions that matter to viewers." The program in question is the CBC's 'flagship' news program Power and Politics.[41]

The intent was obvious. The 'journalist' was hosting the CBC's premier news program to present false

---

[40] Cosmin Dzsurdzsa, "CBC Anchor Invents Conspiracy about Russia Orchestrating Freedom Convoy," True North (True North Centre for Public Policy, January 29, 2022), https://tnc.news/2022/01/29/cbc-anchor-invents-conspiracy-about-russia-orchestrating-freedom-convoy/. **Rated B2**
[41] CBC News Team, "Power & Politics - CBC Media Centre," CBC News (CBC/Radio Canada, 2022), https://www.cbc.ca/mediacentre/program/power-politics . **Not rated**

information intended to create a misleading narrative about the Freedom Convoy 2022.

This is an example of a known approach in propaganda generation techniques – the anchoring bias.[42] This well-studied form of cognitive bias[43] suggests that when people have no knowledge about a subject, they tend to be overly influenced by the first piece of information they receive. Therefore, consumers of news need to be critical thinkers. Many first reports on the news tend to be fragmented or false due to the 'fog of war' situation around breaking news. Critical thinking is even more important when watching stated-funded broadcasters such as the CBC, RT, Al Jazeera, or Xinhua.

Directed and Manipulated by Foreign Agents

The CBC Power and Politics interview was not a 'one-off' event. It was part of a pattern of events that used baseless allegations to push the Russian foreign influence theme.

Harry Forestell[44] of the CBC ran an interview with the title of *Convoy protesters manipulated by foreign*

---

[42] Editors, "Why We Tend to Rely Heavily upon the First Piece of Information We Receive - Anchoring Bias Explained," The Decision Lab, 2022, https://thedecisionlab.com/biases/anchoring-bias. **Rated B1**

[43] Charlotte Ruhl, "What Is Cognitive Bias?" What Is Cognitive Bias? | Simply Psychology (Simply Scholar Ltd, May 4, 2021), https://www.simplypsychology.org/cognitive-bias.html. **Rated B1**

[44] Harry Forestell and David Shipley, "Convoy Protesters Manipulated by Foreign Agents, Says Cybersecurity Expert," CBC News (CBC/Radio Canada, 2002),

agents, says cybersecurity expert. The 3:29 interview contained a series of allegations offered with no evidence other than suppositions.

The interview starts with Mr. Forestell making the following statement:

> *"Even after two weeks of chaos, it is still unclear exactly who is behind the so-called truckers convoy. But it is clear that they are well connected as police in Ottawa clamped down on Parliament Hill other protests began popping up in Ontario and elsewhere."*

Consider the opening statement. Mr. Forestell suggests it is unclear who is behind the convoy two weeks after it has arrived in Ottawa. But (allegedly) lacking such information, Mr. Forestell is certain that other protest movements across the country are "well connected."

The nationwide showings of support and other protests were not connected in any organizational sense. The backing for the Freedom Convoy was an indicator of the widespread popular support among Canadians. It was not, as the interview would go on to suggest, the result of foreign influence.

Nonetheless, the CBC broadcast opens with the idea that 'correlation is causation' without providing any evidence to support the claim. Like so many other CBC and mainstream media news reports, it starts the report with a false statement, presents it as reality, and then builds on the initial deceit.

---

https://www.cbc.ca/player/play/2002191939918 . **Rated D4**

The interview then goes on to introduce a 'cyber expert' who then suggests that the truckers protesting vaccine mandates in Canada were being "directed" and "manipulated by foreign agents."

The cyber expert offered no evidence as to how he concluded that foreign influence was behind the Freedom Convoy. He then asks a rhetorical question and provides his answer:

> "Who would have reason right now to cause as much chaos in Canada as possible? Well, top of that list is Russia. We are actively engaged in a geopolitical battle about the future of the Ukraine."

The cyber expert followed with:

> "When I narrow down my list of suspects, and I don't have enough evidence to win in a court of law, but I don't need that right now. This smacks of the kind of moves that Russia has made in the past to the United States and continues to do around the world."

It is worthy of note that the cyber expert says that this kind of move "smacks" of the moves that Russia has made in the past in the United States. In his mind, and that of the CBC, it is valid to accuse Canadian citizens of being under the influence of foreign operatives in Russia because it "smacks" of what he believes are similar operations in the USA. While it is an entirely separate discussion, it is noteworthy that after years of claims in the USA that the Russians have been behind a variety of malfeasance issues, those claims have been debunked.

The cyber expert also stated that the creation of the large Facebook groups to "foster communication among hundreds of thousands of people" was the "Russian internet research agency playbook." This claim was offered, as with the others, with no evidence other than that it fits with his idea of a mythical Russian playbook.

Other References

Multiple other individuals and organizations made statements concerning foreign intervention controlling the convoy following the CBC reporting. For instance, one self-identified former Liberal Party candidate stated on social media that:

> "There has been an increasing amount of disturbing information related to possible foreign influence of the trucker convoy and illegal sieges of cities like Ottawa. Democracy is precious and we must do everything to protect it. I want to know exactly who is behind this."[45]

International Response – Conspiracy Theories

---

[45] Tyler Watt (@tylerwatt90), "There Has Been an Increasing Amount of Disturbing Information Related to Possible Foreign Influence of the Trucker Convoy and Illegal Sieges of Cities like Ottawa." Twitter.com, February 11, 2022, https://twitter.com/tylerwatt90/status/14923241379262873 64 . **Not Rated.**

The CBC's claim of Russian interference was mocked by other news agencies. The UK-based Daily Mail posted the rather lengthy headline which stated:

> *"Canada's state broadcaster spreads bizarre conspiracy theory that 'Russian actors' are behind 50,000-strong 'Freedom Convoy' of truckers protesting Justin Trudeau's vaccine mandate"* [46]

The Daily Mail stated that the CBC was Canada's foremost broadcaster and that it was "spreading a conspiracy theory that 'Russian actors' are behind the 'Freedom Convoy' trucker vaccine mandate protests."

The True North also reported on the CBC story with a headline that read *CBC anchor invents conspiracy about Russia orchestrating freedom convoy.* [47]

A Non-Correction Correction

On the 3rd of February 2022, the CBC 'clarified' its claim that the Kremlin was behind the Freedom Convoy protest at Parliament Hill. The claim was not factual, according to CBC, but they then added that the claim "should have referenced experts' concerns that during

---

[46] Alex Hammer, "CBC Spreading Conspiracy Theory That 'Russian Actors' Are behind Trucker Vaccine Mandate Protests," Daily Mail Online (Associated Newspapers Ltd, February 2, 2022), https://www.dailymail.co.uk/news/article-10468751/CBC-spreading-conspiracy-theory-Russian-actors-trucker-vaccine-mandate-protests.html. **Rated C3.**

[47] Cosmin Dzsurdzsa, *"CBC Anchor Invents Conspiracy about Russia Orchestrating Freedom Convoy,"* True North (True North Centre for Public Policy, January 29, 2022). **Rated B2.**

the current tension over Ukraine, Moscow could use its cyber and disinformation capabilities." The CBC did not provide the basis for their claim of concern. No intelligence or police agency in Canada has suggested that the Russians were somehow fueling the process.[48]

Assessment

One report with no evidence shows a lack of journalistic standards with no editorial overview. More than one report suggests a pattern of the wilful production of false material, especially when the reports are days or weeks apart.

The initial Russian conspiracy theory story was run on the 29th of January 2022. The second story was run on 11 February 2022, some 13 days later. This was *after* the CBC had issued a correction on the initial Russian conspiracy theory story.

In other words, even after the CBC was mocked for running a fake story, they doubled down and produced a second, *evidence-free* story advancing the same false narrative.

The reasons for this are uncertain, but the CBC, as a state broadcaster, has a reputation for defending the Government of Canada and attacking any opposition forces. This runs contrary to the general principle that

---

[48] Editors, "CBC Corrects Kremlin Story," Blacklock's Reporter (1395804 Ontario Ltd, February 4, 2022), https://www.blacklocks.ca/cbc-corrects-kremlin-claim/. **Rated B2.**

the purpose of a free press in a democracy is to hold the government to account.

These events surrounding the Russian conspiracy theory story provide one more piece of evidence that the CBC is more interested in supporting the Liberal Party government than they are in journalist integrity.

As another reminder, all of this was occurring before the Russian invasion of Ukraine which did not occur before the 24th of February 2022.

CHAPTER 6: THE FIRST EVENT AND RACISM

From the outset, the Freedom Convoy 2022 was identified by a variety of politicians and journalists as being racist, misogynist, homophobic, transphobic, antisemitic, violent, arsonists, rapists, conspiracy theorists, white supremacists, Nazis, terrorists, and Islamophobes. NDP leader Jagmeet Singh said that the convoy was led by those that claim the superiority of the white blood line.[49]

The convoy was also accused of being anti-vaxxers, which was manifestly false. Many of those at the center of the convoy were double vaccinated. The Freedom Convoy was never about vaccinations; it was about forced mandates.

In short, any pejorative word or phrase that could be found was thrown at the Freedom Convoy.

This was not a new experience for many Canadians. The politics of identity have been a crucial part of the governing process put into place by Prime Minister Trudeau. Any who holds contrary views to him, or his advisors such as Gerald Butts, have been called Nazis,

---

[49] Jagmeet Singh, *"Today We Commemorate 5 Years since a Terrorist Attacked and Murdered Muslims in a Quebec City Mosque. we Said Never Again and,* Today Conservative MPs Have Endorsed a Convoy Led by Those That Claim the Superiority of the White Bloodline and Equate Islam to a Disease.," Twitter (Twitter Inc., January 29, 2022), https://twitter.com/theJagmeetSingh/status/1487478167652 773888. **Not Rated.**

racists, misogynists, and other insulting terms. Like many progressives or globalists, he is frequently unable to support his views and ideas, so he falls back on name-calling. As with many others who practice the politics of identity, Prime Minister Trudeau (and much of the mainstream media) operates by placing false labels on individuals and then attacking them for what those labels represent.

Speaking on the 1st of February 2022, Prime Minister Trudeau stated that:

> *"Today in the House, Members of Parliament unanimously condemned the antisemitism, Islamophobia, anti-Black racism, homophobia, and transphobia that we've seen on display in Ottawa over the past number of days. Together, let's keep working to make Canada more inclusive."*[50]

In a Hillary Clinton 'deplorables' moment, Prime Minister Trudeau also called the convoy a fringe element with unacceptable views that do not represent the views of Canadians.[51] It should be noted that this

---

[50] Justin Trudeau, "Today in the House, Members of Parliament Unanimously Condemned the Antisemitism, Islamophobia, Anti-Black Racism, Homophobia, and Transphobia That We've Seen on Display in Ottawa over the Past Number of Days. Together, Let's Keep Working to Make Canada More Inclusive.," Twitter (Twitter Inc., February 1, 2022), https://twitter.com/JustinTrudeau/status/1488660359422648320. **Not Rated.**

[51] Editors, *"Trudeau Says 'Fringe Minority' in Trucker Convoy with 'Unacceptable Views' Don't Represent Canadians,"*

comment was made on the 27th of January 2022 before the Freedom Convoy had even arrived in Ottawa.

It would be an impossible task to assess all the hate-filled commentary that was flung at the Freedom Convoy and assess it individually. That would be a rather large book unto itself.

However, a few quick observations can be made to dispel the most vicious and untrue accusations.

The First Event of Freedom Convoy 2022

A spiritual service was held on the 30th of January 2022 on Wellington Street directly in front of the Parliament buildings. This was the first formal event of Freedom Convoy 2022.

The event's speakers consisted of the following persons:

- A clan mother of the Dene Clan from the Northwest Territories;
- A clan mother of the Cree Tribe;
- A male Jewish truck driver/podcaster from Toronto;
- A Metis woman from Alberta;
- A black French-speaking evangelical minister from Montreal, and
- A white Mennonite preacher.

Global News (Corus Entertainment Inc. Corus News, January 27, 2022), https://globalnews.ca/video/8542159/trudeau-says-fringe-minority-in-trucker-convoy-with-unacceptable-views-dont-represent-canadians. **Rated B3.**

The event was endorsed by an Arabic Shia Muslim Imam (@imamofpeace) who was born in Iraq, educated in Iran, and living in Australia.

As can be seen, the Freedom Convoy's lineup of speakers is considerably more diverse than most Canadian gatherings and represented support from a wide range of communities.

While the Freedom Convoy would come under constant attacks from Jagmeet Singh, the leader of the NDP, a variety of Sikhs and Sikh groups came out in support of the convoy. They stated that the NDP leader did not represent the Sikh community on this issue.

There are no words to describe the vicious lies being spewed from Jagmeet Singh's mouth regarding the people in the convoy to Ottawa, and the Sikh community is being loud and clear that Jagmeet's lies do NOT represent them or their thoughts.[52]

As Sikhs for Truth stated: *"The freedom convoy has nothing to do with "race, or health, or Nazi flags, or masks, but rather keeping future children off of a biometric digital ID wallet system that will control every aspect of their lives."*[53]

---

[52] Odessa Orlewicz, "Jan 30 - the Sikh Community Fights Back against NDP Leader Jagmeet Singh's Lies & Deception About Convoy," Librti.com (Liberty Talk Canada, January 30, 2022), https://librti.com/page/view-video?id=1675. **Not Rated.**
[53] Sikhs for Truth, 11 February 2022. The statement can be seen at
https://threadreaderapp.com/thread/149209813446551552

There is No Racism Here

Three Sikhs from the Toronto area were interviewed in Ottawa about why they were involved in the Ottawa protest. Their primary message was that NDP leader Jagmeet Singh does not represent the Sikh people on this issue. During the interview they stated:[54,55]

> *We want to get back to the freedom... it is not about health anymore... you give them an inch and they will take a mile... we got batons in our ribs... we were holding the line and talking to the police and we got batons in our ribs and punched in the face... we had to remove some of the elderly because they were being trampled... the police were being extra aggressive... this is not about health anymore... they are taking our freedoms... we are citizens and we want to be free... they are seizing banks accounts just because you donated to the convoy – you live in a free country. My ancestors were POWs in Hitler's camps. Sikhs were born to face oppression and basically fight against tyranny...* **we want the public to know there is no racism here.** *Indigenous people... people from all walks of life. If we do not*

6.html .

[54] Unknown, "Canadian Sikhs Have a Message for @JustinTrudeau and @Thejagmeetsingh," Rumble.com, February 19, 2022, https://rumble.com/vvcmay-canadian-sikhs-have-a-message-for-justintrudeau-and-thejagmeetsingh.html. **Not Rated.**

[55] Raven Dark Media, "Sikh Community Speaks In Ottawa," YouTube (Google LLC, February 18, 2022), https://www.youtube.com/?gl=NL. **Not Rated.**

hold the line now... in a nation like Canada, this kind of tyranny can take place... **Jagmeet Singh is a complete scumbag.** *Guess what — they are involved... They are the ones closing down people's bank accounts... we would like everyone to know that* **Jagmeet Singh does not represent the Sikhs and he never did.** (Emphasis added)

Assessment

Most of the accusations against the Freedom Convoy, especially those made before the convoy's arrival in Ottawa were simply manufactured by politicians and others. As with many other narratives, it seems they had more to do with a determined effort to undermine Freedom Convoy 2022 rather than an assessment of the nature and intent of the convoy.

The accusations, especially those coming from political leaders such as Justin Trudeau and Jagmeet Singh, should be seen through the lens of their adherence to a globalist and progressive ideology.

CHAPTER 7: ARSON

On 6 February 2022, an attempted arson occurred against an Ottawa apartment building. According to news reports, the front doors of the apartment building had been forced closed and sealed with tape. Fire starter bricks had been placed in the front lobby. A passerby spotted the fire; forced open the door and extinguished the fire before it spread.[56] This occurred on the 10th day of the Freedom Convoy protest.

No evidence linking the Freedom Convoy to the event was produced at the time of the event nor in the following days. Nonetheless, a wide range of politicians and 'journalists' produced statements blaming the Freedom Convoy.

The fake claims put forth about the relationship between the Freedom Convoy and the arson were useful to the Government of Canada. They "offered a very convenient contributing pretext for the declaration of the Emergencies Act."[57]

---

[56] Ted Raymond, "Suspect Charged in Downtown Ottawa Arson Last Month Not Connected with 'Freedom Convoy': Police," CTV News Ottawa (Bell Media, March 21, 2022), https://ottawa.ctvnews.ca/suspect-charged-in-downtown-ottawa-arson-last-month-not-connected-with-freedom-convoy-police-1.5828171. **Rated C3**.

[57] Rex Murphy, "Will Anyone Apologize for Falsely Accusing Truckers of Attempted Arson in Ottawa?," National Post (Postmedia Network Inc., April 8, 2022), https://nationalpost.com/opinion/rex-murphy-will-anyone-apologize-for-falsely-accusing-truckers-of-attempted-arson-

Among the headlines and statements from politicians were:

- OPS investigating arson case after viral tweets allege "Freedom Convoy" protester involvement[58]
- Opposition Leader Jagmeet Singh stated that *"This convoy protest is not a peaceful protest.... Violence is commonplace. We saw an example of this violence with an attempted arson of a downtown apartment building, where people started a fire and taped the doors closed when they exited. I ask members to take a moment to think what that means. They had the forethought to set a fire and then tape the doors so no one could escape. This is not isolated. There are ongoing examples."*
- One comment from Ottawa Mayor Jim Watson about the Freedom Convoy and the arson attempt was *"Show human decency and leave our community now that you've made your point."*[59]

---

in-ottawa. **Rated B2.**

[58] Imaan Sheikh, "OPS Investigating Arson Case after Viral Tweets Allege 'Freedom Convoy' Protester Involvement," DH News (Buzz Connected Media Inc., February 7, 2022), https://dailyhive.com/vancouver/ottawa-police-arson-investigation-freedom-convoy. **Rated D3.**

[59] Amanda Connolly, "Police Arson Unit Probing Alleged Attempt to Start Fire in Ottawa Apartment Building, Says Mayor," Global News (Corus Entertainment Inc. - Corus News., February 8, 2022), https://globalnews.ca/news/8600592/trucker-convoy-police-

- Another statement from Mayor Watson made to the Ottawa City Council was that the arson attempt "clearly demonstrates the malicious intent" of the truckers' convoy on Parliament Hill.[60] Of note, this was one day after the arson attempt where the investigation had not had a chance to even get started.
- Multiple Members of Parliament also made false statements assigning blame for the arson to the Freedom Convoy. Among them were Sameer Zuberi (Lib.), Matthew Green (NDP), Arif Virani (Lib.), Francisco Sorbara (Lib.), Alistair MacGregor (NDP), Anita Vandenbeld (Lib.), Laurel Collins (NDP), Ron McKinnon (Lib.), Jennifer O'Connell (Lib.), Ryan Turnbull (Lib.), Parm Bains (Lib.), Jenny Kwan (NDP), Andy Fillmore (Lib.), Peter Schlefke (Lib.) and Gord Johns (NDP).[61]

---

investigating-arson-apartment/. **Rated D3**.

[60] Cosmin Dzsurdzsa, "No Evidence of Terrorist Activity during Convoy Protests: RCMP Financial Crime Director," TNC.news (True North Centre for Public Policy, March 17, 2022), https://tnc.news/2022/03/17/no-evidence-of-terrorist-activity-during-convoy-protests-rcmp-financial-crime-director/. **Rated B2**.

[61] Cosmin Dzsurdzsa, "DZSURDZSA: How the Liberals and NDP Pushed the Arson Hoax about the Freedom Convoy," True North (True North Centre for Public Policy, April 7, 2022), https://tnc.news/2022/04/07/dzsurdzsa-how-the-liberals-and-ndp-pushed-the-arson-hoax-about-the-freedom-convoy/. **Rated B2**.

- Global News reporter Ross Lord stated he spoke with an unidentified woman who allegedly stated she heard one of the arsonists say "I am a protestor. I support the protest."[62]

The above examples are a limited sample. A full list of the social media, political and mainstream media commentary would fill pages of a book.

What is clear, however, is that all these statements were false. A reasonable assessment can be made that many of them were either malicious or willfully ignorant.

Two individuals were eventually arrested for the attempted arson. In both cases, the Ottawa Police stated that neither individual had any connection to the Freedom Convoy.[63]

Willful Lies from Public Safety Minster Mendicino

The Minister for Public Safety is responsible for overseeing the internal security departments of the Government of Canada. This includes responsibility for

---

[62] Amanda Connolly, "Police Arson Unit Probing Alleged Attempt to Start Fire in Ottawa Apartment Building, Says Mayor," Global News (Corus Entertainment Inc. - Corus News., February 8, 2022), https://globalnews.ca/news/8600592/trucker-convoy-police-investigating-arson-apartment/. **Rated D3.**

[63] Media Relations Section, "Second Man Charged in February Lisgar Street Arson Investigation," Ottawa Police Service (City of Ottawa, April 6, 2022), https://www.ottawapolice.ca/Modules/News/index.aspx?newsId=46eea503-f886-4e7a-9188-edbecabca0a6. **Not rated.**

the Correctional Service of Canada, the Royal Canadian Mounted Police, the Parole Board of Canada, the Canada Border Services Agency, and the Canadian Security Intelligence Service.

As such, the Minister of Public Safety is essentially the chief law enforcement officer for all of Canada.

When testifying in a parliamentary committee on the 26th of April 2022, the Minster referred to Freedom Convoy 2022. He was referring to a February 6th attempted arson in Ottawa and made the following statement:[64]

> *"When people who live in apartment buildings find that their front doors are locked, and fires are set in the hallways and corridors..."[65]*

At that point, Minister Mendicino was interrupted by Member of Parliament Glenn Motz on a point of order. He stated:

> *"Point of order, Mr. Speaker. That statement right there has been proven false by the Ottawa Police Service and there is no connection to the protestors*

---

[64] Editors, "False Convoy Claim Repeated," Blacklock's Reporter, April 27, 2022, https://www.blacklocks.ca/false-convoy-claim-repeated/. **Rated B2.**

[65] Sarah Fischer, "@GlenMotz Calls out @Marcomendicino for Attempting to Mislead a Parliamentary Committee by Spreading Fake News! #Cdnpoli #EmergenciesAct," Twitter (Twitter, Inc., April 26, 2022), https://twitter.com/SarahFischer__/status/15191009174460 62083. **Not rated.**

whatsoever and for this minister to suggest that is absolutely unacceptable in this committee."

It can be seen in this exchange that the Minister of Public Safety is willfully lying to Parliament and the country. He is attempting to prop up a fake allegation that he knows has been proven false.

Social Media as a Basis for Investigation

One disturbing aspect of the entire arson misinformation event was the impact of social media. A claim, made by an individual on social media was given credence. The claim is dubious at best and directly contradicts the investigational conclusions of the Ottawa Police Force.

Nonetheless, it served as the basis for a variety of stories and helped fuel the fake news response. The failing here is not that social media allows such statements. This can fall under the heading of free speech. The problem is that a wide range of individuals, many of whom should know better, used this as a basis for their false claims.

For the record, the following paragraphs represent a series of social media statements put out by the person in question.

> *"I've been hesitating to post this publicly, but I feel I must for the safety of downtown Ottawa residents. Here are the facts: Last night two arsonists brought a full package of fire starter bricks into our building's lobby at 5 am. The building is located at Metcalfe & Lisgar. We were able to see the*

building's video footage of the event. These two men got into the lobby and began lighting the full package. The building is old and has wood paneling on the walls. It is also located at the epicentre of the convoy protests in Ottawa's core. One of them taped up the door handles so no one could get in or out. This is the most insidious part of the experience besides the lighting of the fire. After a night of blaring horns and fireworks until 4 am, some residents had yelled & pleaded with protesters outside to stop.

As the fire was being lit, a tenant walked by and nervously asked who they were. One admitted being part of the convoy protests. The tenant quickly got into the elevator and arsonists continued to ignite the package. Once lit, it grew and nearly touched the wood panel walls. The arsonists escaped out the side door as the video shows the fire growing. After speaking with many residents, it became clear that certain protesters outside became very aggressive and angry at the tenants in the hours leading up to the arson. Not all protesters, but a few screamed and were clearly upset by the confrontation earlier in the night. A good Samaritan was walking by the door outside and saw the fire. Luckily the door opened after some struggle with the taped handles, he got in and was able to extinguish the flames. It is clear to us, as residents, that this was a blatant reprisal by protesters. Not only have they subjected Ottawa residents to widespread harassment, assault, and aggression, but now an attempt to light an entire building on fire. Our hope is that the @OttawaPolice and @JimWatsonOttawa will [heed] @cmckenney's calls for an immediate and firm resolution to the convoy's occupation. This incident could have ended much, much worse. For anyone wondering how I got the footage, the building manager is a cool dude, and let us see it. Police were called once the fire remnants were noticed in the morning and they are investigating. Also, the tenant who interacted with the arsonists did file a report. Police are pulling it all together and taking statements from tenants in the building. I will also add that the cameras are well hidden."

Assessment

The arson accusation and following media frenzy are a near-perfect example of what is crippling trust in the Canadian Government and the mainstream media. A false story was broadcast, then repeatedly used to support the equally false narrative that the Freedom Convoy was a violent organization.

Taken in isolation, this type of false and defamatory information is serious. However, taken in the context of the overall behaviour of individuals such as Mayor Jim Watson of Ottawa and the Honourable Jagmeet Singh, leader of the federal NDP, it is reasonable to assess malice driven by a political agenda.

Further to that, it is clear that the Government of Canada, in the person of the Public Safety Minister, has attempted to keep this false narrative alive by lying to Parliament about the issue. Despite being aware that his statement was false, the minister took one more opportunity to make a false statement to slander the convoy.

Additionally, this case is another nail in the coffin of the mainstream media and the political classes in Ottawa.

CHAPTER 8: LOADED SHOTGUNS

One of the most repeated false narratives about Freedom Convoy 2022 was that the police found "loaded shotguns" and other weapons while searching trucks in Ottawa. For instance, the Toronto Star published a story on 19 March 2022 that stated "Fears that there were weapons inside some of the trucks proved prescient. A police source said loaded shotguns were found." The story also quoted Public Safety Minister Marco Mendicino as remarking "it was 'nothing short of miraculous' that nobody was seriously injured."[66,67]

This was yet another attempt to highlight Freedom Convoy 2022 as violent and to provide a pretext for the Emergencies Act.

As with most of the other narratives, it was false. No shotguns were found – loaded or not. No other firearms were found in the search of trucks in Ottawa. It

---

[66] Editors, "Convoy Claims Contradicted," Blacklock's Reporter (1395804 Ontario Ltd, March 25, 2022),
https://www.blacklocks.ca/convoy-claims-contradicted/.
Rated B2.
[67] Justin Ling, "Was It Really about Vaccine Mandates - or Something Darker? The inside Story of the Convoy Protests," Toronto Star (Toronto Star Newspapers Ltd., March 19, 2022), The story is behind a paywall at
https://www.thestar.com/news/canada/2022/03/19/was-it-really-about-vaccine-mandates-or-something-darker-the-inside-story-of-the-convoy-protests.html

appears that the story was manufactured and presented without any evidence.

The report of loaded shotguns was based on the ever-elusive "police source." The public does not know who – if anyone – made the claim. The public will likely never know if the particular "police source" had access to real intelligence or was simply reporting information that s/he had heard through a police grapevine. In other words, this reporting, from both a journalistic and intelligence perspective, is a complete failure. The consumer of the information has no way of knowing the source reliably or the information credibility of the issue at hand.

Parliamentary Committee

The fake narrative about the presence of loaded shotguns in the Freedom Convoy fell apart during a session of a parliamentary committee.

Ottawa Police Service (Interim) Chief Steve Bell was called to testify to a parliamentary committee on 18 March 2022. After taking over as the third Ottawa police chief during Freedom Convoy 2022, he was at the forefront of clearing out the protests.

During the committee proceedings, Chief Bell was asked if any guns were found in trucks that were part of the Freedom Convoy. His responses to the question reveal, once again, the deceitful and devious nature of the officials connected to government activities around the Freedom Convoy.

The Member of Parliament asking the questions was Dane Lloyd. Due to the evasive nature of Chief Bell, he was forced to repeatedly ask about the number of guns found by the police. The question-and-answer session took the following path[68]:

MP Dane: In Ottawa during the protest clearing operation were any loaded shotguns found in the trucks of protestors?

Chief Bell: Mr. Chair what I can indicate is throughout the protest, we did receive information and intelligence around weapons and possession of weapons by people that either had attended or intended on attending the occupation. As a result of the clearing, at no point did we make any firearm-related charges, yet there are investigations that continue in relation to weapons possession at the occupation.

MP Dane: I guess, yes or no, Interim Chief – were loaded firearms found in the trucks during the protest clearing operation? Yes, or no?

Chief Bell: As I had indicated Mr. Chair, there have been no charges laid to date in relation to weapons at the occupation site.

---

[68] Dane Lloyd, "Ottawa Police Confirm No Firearms Found during Clearing of Convoy Protests," YouTube (Google LLC, March 24, 2022), The full exchange between MP Dane Lloyd and Ottawa Interim Police Chief Bell can be seen online at https://www.youtube.com/watch?v=F_zQe4pCk30. Not rated.

MP Dane: It's just a clear question, Interim Chief. Were weapons found? Were loaded firearms found? Yes, or no?

Chief Bell: No, not relating to any charges at this point.

MP Dane: Thank you Interim Chief, that is very illuminating. On March 19th, this past Saturday, a reporter Justin Ling wrote in the Toronto Star that police sources indicated that loaded shotguns were found in trucks at the Ottawa protest. Is this false information?

Chief Bell: So, I am unfamiliar with the quote you are referring to but as I indicated before we have received intelligence information, continued criminal investigations and no charges have been laid to date.

MP Dane: But the article claims that a police source told the journalist that loaded shotguns were found in trucks during the protest clearing operation and you have said to this committee that this is in fact not the case – that loaded shotguns were not found in trucks during the clearing operation. Is that the case Interim Chief?

Chief Bell: Thank you for the question. Mr. Chair, as I indicated, we received intelligence information. I'm unclear around the source the information was received for that article or the corroboration around it, but we have not laid any charges in relation ... (At this point, MP Danes cuts off the Chief's answer.)

MP Dane: ...Ok Interim Chief. Can you clarify Interim Chief, speaking on the record and not off the record that loaded shotguns were not found in the vehicles during the protest operations. Can you confirm that?

Chief Bell. So yes, consistent with my answer previously, Yes, I do confirm to date...

MP Dane ...Thank you.

Chief Bell: ...that no charges have been laid...

Member of Parliament Dane concluded his statements to the committed by stating:

"We had a cabinet minister, the Minister of Crown-Indigenous Relations Marc Miller, retweet this article from Justin Ling from the Toronto Star claiming there were loaded shotguns found in trucks. This is misinformation, Chief, and I would submit to the committee, misinformation being spread by a journalist and misinformation being spread by a member of this government."[69]

As can be seen from the above exchange, Chief Bell repeatedly attempted to avoid answering the question about whether loaded shotguns had been found as was reported by the Toronto Star. Instead, he attempted to avoid answering the question through the process of misdirection. Rather than answering yes or no, he created a misdirection by stating that *there are*

---

[69] Editors, "Convoy Claims Contradicted," Blacklock's Reporter (1395804 Ontario Ltd, March 25, 2022) **Rated B2.**

investigations that continue in relation to weapons possession.

His answer was a clear attempt to avoid answering the real question and he did it repeatedly.

The reality is that no guns were found, and the Ottawa Police Chief was finally forced to admit this under repeated and direct questioning.

Assessment

The entire narrative around the finding of loaded shotguns in the Ottawa convoy was false. Like the other narratives, it was first advanced by highly questionable individuals quoting 'sources' that were not identified. Nonetheless, the damage was done. As noted elsewhere in this book, people will often believe the first information they hear about a story.

Furthermore, the spreading of the false narrative by a cabinet minister lent credibility to the false narrative. This story of "loaded shotguns" was part of the narrative used for the imposition of the Emergencies Act. In other words, even though the story was false, it was used to justify one of the most horrific abuses of civil rights in Canada which will damage Canada and its economic stability for years.

N.B.: As of the date of this writing, no one that I am aware of has been held accountable for the spreading of this false information.

N.B.: A separate gun story emerged from the Coutts Crossing protest in Alberta. Although this protest was separate from the Ottawa protest, the narrative was virtually the same. The seizure of the guns was claimed to be a part of the trucker's protest, but the guns were seized from a house and the individuals charged had nothing to do with the local protest.

CHAPTER 9: THREATS OF RAPE

Public Safety Minister Marco Mendicino accused the Freedom Convoy 2022 of issuing rape threats. He did this during a Public Safety committee meeting on 25 February 2022. The Minister also said that threats of rape by political protestors helped justify the Emergencies Act.[70] One of his statements was:

"There were Ottawans who were subjected to intimidation, harassment, threats of rape."[71]

Minister Mendicino's comments during this parliamentary committee hearing were seen as untrustworthy. The threat of rape had not been mentioned once during some forty hours of emergency parliamentary sittings to discuss the implementation of the Emergencies Act.[72]

As Conservative Member of Parliament, Larry Brock stated: "My question to you is very pointed: If that allegation did not result in a criminal charge will you

---

[70] Liz Braun, "Conservative Politicians Question Sexual Assault Threat from Truckers," Toronto Sun (Toronto Sun, a division of Postmedia Network Inc., February 28, 2022), https://torontosun.com/news/national/conservative-politicians-question-sexual-assault-threat-from-truckers. **Rated C3.**

[71] Editors, "Claims Truckers Were Rapists," Blacklock's Reporter, February 28, 2022, https://www.blacklocks.ca/claims-truckers-were-rapists/. **Rated B2.**

[72] Editors, "Claims Truckers Were Rapists," Blacklock's Reporter, February 28, 2022. **Rated B2.**

undertake to provide this committee with proof of the allegation?"[73]

Conservative MP Raquel Dancho also raised the issue of why the Cabinet allowed MPs, senators, reporters, political aides, and the public to walk past the Freedom Convoy blockade over 24 days if protesters were known to be violent criminals. She questioned Minister Mendicino by asking *"Women on this panel right now walked past that protest every day and you are saying there was a threat to public safety? I just don't know you could be saying on one hand this is a national emergency for public safety, and I walked every day past these protests."*[74]

A similar line of questioning towards Minister Mendicino was raised by reporter Rupa Subramanya. She asked a rhetorical question:

> *"I as a female person of colour spent hours talking to truckers and protesters, sometimes late into the night, and not once did I feel unsafe. If it was so dangerous, how do experiences like mine conform with the official narrative?"*[75]

[73] Editors, "Claims Truckers Were Rapists," Blacklock's Reporter, February 28, 2022,
https://www.blacklocks.ca/claims-truckers-were-rapists/.
Rated B2.
[74] Editors, "Claims Truckers Were Rapists," Blacklock's Reporter, February 28, 2022. **Rated B2.**
[75] Rupa Subramanya, "THX for asking the right questions @Raqueldancho. I as a female person of colour spent hours talking to truckers and protesters, sometimes late into the night and not once did I feel unsafe. If it was so dangerous,

One of the first public records of the accusations of sexual assault came from NDP MP Charlie Angus who said he had three messages from women[76] in the Gloucester-Metcalfe Streets area "talking about the threats of rape they are facing because of the lawlessness and lack of police to protect residents in Centretown in Ottawa from this protest." Of note, MP Angus also supported a motion at the same time in the parliament to "investigate how GoFundMe is allowing anonymous sources to funnel money to what may be an extremist action. [77] He provided no evidence or source for these (false) allegations.

It is *possible*, although not provable, that the entire narrative around sexual assault and rape started with one social media posting. An anonymous person stated that a "Freedom trucker guy" was on O'Connor Street at the same time as she was around 12:45 PM (presumably on 29 January 2022). He allegedly told her to take her mask off and when she did not respond, he allegedly said:

---

how do experiences like mine conform with the official narrative?" Twitter (Google LLC, February 28, 2022), https://twitter.com/rupasubramanya/status/1498342415295553538. **Not Rated.**

[76] A search of social media and mainstream media provided no further information on these anonymous sources. They were never identified nor where they asked to provide any sort of statements as far as can be determined.

[77] Charlie Angus, "Debates of Feb. 3rd, 2022," openparliament.ca (Government of Canada, February 3, 2022), https://openparliament.ca/debates/2022/2/3/charlie-angus-2/. **Not Rated.**

"I will come and take more than that mask off if you don't take that s**t off right now." According to this same post, this anonymous person then called the non-emergency police line and was told *"we are aware there are threats being made to those wearing masks our recommendation is not to wear them outside until demonstrators can be removed from the court."*[78]

The Ottawa Police were contacted over this report and stated that they were aware of the social media posting but had received no such report.[79]

(Former) RCMP Corporal Danny Bulford worked closely with the Freedom Convoy 2022. Most of his work was related to security matters and he worked with Police Liaison teams daily. In this situation, he stated:

"He (Minister Mendicino) also made claims about people being threatened with rape by Convoy participants. That information was never

---

[78] Nicole Graves, "This Is Disgusting!! They Need to Leave!!," Twitter (Google LLC, February 1, 2022), https://twitter.com/trvlbug71/status/1488701152564813824 . **Rated D4.**

[79] The Real Andy Lee Show, "Can't Wait for Marco to Be Quizzed on 'Truckers Are Rapists' Claims. As Far as I Can Tell, That Tale Stemmed from This Social Media Post. Here's the Problem: I Contacted Ottawa Police over It. They Issued a Statement Saying They Knew of the Post, but Had Received No Such Report.," Twitter (Google LLC, April 27, 2022), https://twitter.com/RealAndyLeeShow/status/1519338178057957376. **Not Rated.**

communicated to me by the Police Liaison teams despite daily interaction. Highly suspect."[80]

Assessment

No charges were ever laid against anyone connected to the Freedom Convoy concerning rape or sexual assault. No public information has ever shown that investigations were started nor is there any record of a complaint by a citizen.

The entire "truckers are rapists" appears to have been generated by Members of Parliament following one anonymous and unsubstantiated statement about a non-violent incident. It is not clear what motivates them to make such false claims, but perhaps they allow their ideology and agendas to overtake the reality on the ground.

While politicians tried to say that members of the Freedom Convoy were attacking passerbys on the street, the reality was different. Even Ottawa Police Chief Sloly had to admit that street crime fell after the protest started. "There have been no riots, injuries, or deaths," he said.[81]

---

[80] Daniel Bulford, "He Also Made Claims about People Being Threatened with Rape by Convoy Participants. That Information Was Never Communicated to Me by the Police Liaison Teams despite Daily Interaction. Highly Suspect.," Twitter (Google LLC, April 26, 2022), https://twitter.com/BulfordDaniel/status/151915196152595 6609

[81] Editors, "Data Contradict Crime Claim," Blacklock's Reporter, February 4, 2022, https://www.blacklocks.ca/data-

Liberal MP Yasir Naqvi (Ottawa Centre) told the House of Commons that "Firecrackers have been hurled at people wearing masks who are simply passing by." As with many of the comments from himself and others such as Liberal MP Mark Holland, such statements are false.

Individuals such as Public Safety Minister Marco Mendicino continue to lie to Parliament on this and other false allegations even after they have been publicly disproved. From this, it can be reasonably concluded that the Government of Canada, through its MPs and Ministers, attempted to create a false narrative to cover up their failings while discrediting Freedom Convoy 2022.

contradict-crime-claim/. **Rated B2**.

CHAPTER 10: TERRORISTS

One of the most egregious narratives against the Freedom Convoy 2022 was that it was funded, in part, by terrorist money and that there were terrorists in the movement.

These claims were used, in part, to justify the use of the Emergencies Act which allowed the Government of Canada to freeze the assets of protesters and donors by applying terrorism and money laundering rules.[82]

For example, New Democratic Party Member of Parliament Alistair MacGregor read out Section 83.01 of the Criminal Code in accusing truckers of terrorism in opposing vaccine mandates:

> *"Our Criminal Code has a definition of terrorism which is 'an act committed in whole or in part for a political, religious or ideological purpose, objective or cause with the intention of intimidating the public,'" said MacGregor. "Activities recognized as criminal within this content can include significant property damage and interference or disruption of essential services, facilities or systems, which I think any casual observer looking at Ottawa right now could probably make a link."*[83]

---

[82] Cosmin Dzsurdzsa, "No Evidence of Terrorist Activity during Convoy Protests: RCMP Financial Crime Director," TNC.news (True North Centre for Public Policy, March 17, 2022), https://tnc.news/2022/03/17/no-evidence-of-terrorist-activity-during-convoy-protests-rcmp-financial-crime-director/. **Rated B2.**

Liberal Party Member of Parliament Tabeeb Noormohamed compared the funding raising for Freedom Convoy 2022 to terrorist financing. When asked why it was necessary to reveal the names of donors to the convoy, he said it was "for the same reason we track terrorist financing."[84]

Ottawa City Councillor Diane Dean referred to the Freedom Convoy as terrorists who were torturing residents. After such initial comments, she repeated the terrorist accusation by stating the efforts to remove her from the Ottawa Police Services Board were "*an opportunity to try and deflect away from the mayor, who made in my estimation just a horrendous decision to negotiate with terrorists.*"[85] The councilor also referred to the Freedom Convoy as "treason" and "an insurrection." She also stated it was a "group of well-polished professional people that are trying to overthrow the government." She also added that "The

---

[83] Editors, "Likens Truckers to Terrorists," Blacklock's Reporter, February 11, 2022, https://www.blacklocks.ca/likens-truckers-to-terrorists/. **Rated B2.**

[84] Cosmin Dzsurdzsa, "Liberal MP Compares Freedom Convoy Funding to 'Terrorist Financing,'" True North (True North Centre for Public Policy, February 4, 2022), https://tnc.news/2022/02/04/liberal-mp-compares-freedom-convoy-funding-to-terrorist-financing/. **Rated B2.**

[85] Kate Porter and Joanne Chianello, "Diane Deans Ousted from Police Services Board by 15 Members of Council | CBC News," CBC News Ottawa (CBC/Radio Canada, February 17, 2022), https://www.cbc.ca/news/canada/ottawa/police-chief-diane-deans-1.6354150. **Rated C2.**

money is flowing from the US. This is right out of the Trump playbook."[86]

Despite her position as a City Councillor who sits on the Police Services Board, Councillor Dean offered no evidence of anyone in the Freedom Convoy movement who was a terrorist or supported terrorist causes. This kind of behaviour was, unfortunately, common throughout the Freedom Convoy protest.

Of note, Councillor Dean was removed from the Police Services Board of the City Council of Ottawa. While complicated, it appears that she was removed for hiring a new police chief without telling the mayor or the rest of the City Council. It also appears that there were long-standing feuds between herself and others. Her view was that she was ousted for not backing the Mayor of Ottawa on his positions vis-à-vis convoy negotiations.[87] However, there is nothing to show she was removed for making fake claims about the Freedom Convoy being terrorists.

---

[86] Cosmin Dzsurdzsa, "Ottawa Councillor and Police Chair Calls Convoy 'Treason' and 'Insurrection,'" True North (True North Centre for Public Policy, February 8, 2022), https://tnc.news/2022/02/08/ottawa-councillor-and-police-chair-calls-convoy-treason-and-insurrection/. **Rated B2**.

[87] Andrew Duffy and Elizabeth Payne, "Former Police Board Chair Diane Deans Says She Was Ousted for Not Backing Mayor's Protester Negotiations," Ottawa Citizen (Postmedia Network Inc., February 18, 2022), https://ottawacitizen.com/news/local-news/former-police-board-chair-says-she-was-ousted-for-not-backing-mayors-protester-negotiations. **Rated B2**.

Terrorism Evidence

On 7 March 2022, Royal Canadian Mounted Police's Director of Financial Crime Denis Beaudoin told the Commons Finance Committee "that there was no evidence of terrorist activity in the funding of the freedom convoy protest."

This statement was in line with that of the Financial Transactions and Reports Analysis Centre of Canada (FINTRAC). When testifying to the House of Commons Finance Committee, Deputy Director Barry MacKillop stated that there was no terrorism money in the convoy's donations. "It was their own money. It wasn't cash that funded terrorism or was in any way money laundering."[88]

Deputy Director MacKillop also stated that he did not find the nature of crowdfunding suspicious in this case. "These were people who supported the cause before it was declared illegal," he stated. "There were people around the world who were fed up with COVID and were upset and saw the demonstrations. I believe they just wanted to support the cause." [89]

Terrorism Charges

---

[88] Editors, "Calls Convoy Cash Harmless," Blacklock's Reporter, February 25, 2022, https://www.blacklocks.ca/calls-convoy-cash-harmless/. **Rated B2.**

[89] Editors, "Calls Convoy Cash Harmless," Blacklock's Reporter, February 25, 2022. **Rated B2.**

No one from the Freedom Convoy was ever charged with a terrorist-related event. There is also no evidence to suggest that any police service operating in or around the Ottawa freedom convoy ever had a functioning investigation into a potential terrorist charge.

The only persons involved in the entire protest movement in Ottawa who had connections to extremism or terrorism were on the government side.

Assessment

While the mainstream media was complicit in advancing the narrative around the Freedom Convoy and terrorism, the majority of influencers in this case were politicians.

The use of the term terrorism, with no evidence, appears to be founded in two areas. The first was to disparage the Freedom Convoy in any way possible. The baseless accusations of terrorism were useful in that respect.

The other area was the Emergencies Act. According to Deputy Prime Minister and Finance Minister Freeland, the Emergencies Act would "broaden the scope of Canada's anti-money laundering and terrorist financing rules so that they cover crowdfunding platforms and the payment service providers they use."[90]

---

[90] Cosmin Dzsurdzsa, "Trudeau Invokes Emergencies Act to Quash Canada-Wide Trucker Protests," True North (True North Centre for Public Policy, February 14, 2022), https://tnc.news/2022/02/14/trudeau-invokes-emergencies-act-to-quash-canada-wide-trucker-protests/. **Rated B2**.

As can be seen, the Government of Canada was using rules governing terrorism financing to seize the bank accounts, freeze credit cards, and halt the payments systems of Canadians who supported the Freedom Convoy. To do this, they needed to generate a narrative around terrorism to justify this action.

CHAPTER 11: ANARCHISTS

The Freedom Convoy 2022 movement had a variety of false narratives generated around it. Many were easily dismissed, such as the CBC's attempt to suggest the convoy was under the control of President Putin of Russia. Other accusations, such as those connected to terrorism were significant in that the Government of Canada used these narratives to justify the imposition of the Emergencies Act.

The most absurd of all the accusations, however, came from a source who should have known better than to make unsubstantiated and nonsensical claims.

Senator Bev Busson (B.C.) is a former Commissioner of the Royal Canadian Mounted Police. As such, she should have a knowledge base that extends to different forms of criminality and threats to national security.

According to Senator Busson, the Freedom Convoy movement had been subverted not long after it emerged. In a statement on 23 February 2022 to the Senate of Canada regarding the "Motion to Confirm the Declaration of a Public Order Emergency," she stated:

> *"Truckers and their supporters gathered in Ottawa on or about January 29 to rally against mask mandates, lockdowns, restrictions on gatherings and other COVID-19 preventive measures. These peaceful protesters, comprised of Canadian citizens exercising the right to demonstrate, soon found their cause co-opted by a much darker element in*

our society. Call them what you will but know that they stand for the overthrow of our government and the dissolution of our democracy."[91] (Emphasis added)

The statement of Senator Busson was offered without any evidence or explanation of what constitutes a "darker element in our society." Whoever these mysterious elements were, however, she was quite clear that they stood for overthrowing the government and dissolving democracy.

The Senator then continued with the following:

"Those in Ottawa were the hardest hit, but the entire country has felt the sting of this lawlessness and disrespect as we watched the nation's capital be turned into an amusement park for <u>anarchists</u>. Make no mistake, their mission remains the dismantling of our government and replacing it with one of their own. Sorry senators, we're not going to be running the country with the Governor General any time soon. <u>These people, by definition, are anarchists. They are professionally led, well funded and skillfully planning the downfall of our democracy</u>. They use children as human shields to obstruct enforcement."

---

[91] Senator Bev Busson, "Topic Intervention 570326 - 1," Senate of Canada (Parliament of Canada, February 23, 2022), https://sencanada.ca/en/senators/busson-bev/interventions/570326/1#hID. **Rated C2**.

No other assessment of her statement can be made other than to say it is bizarre. The majority of those in the Freedom Convoy were small business owners who operated small fleets of trucks. They were taxpaying businesspersons. A variety of others who helped were ex-military, ex-police, and ex-paramedics.

At no point anywhere in Ottawa was it seen that 'anarchists' were operating within the Freedom Convoy. There were no black flags, no anarcho-syndicalism literature, or anarcho-environmental advocacy within Freedom Convoy 2022. There was no discussion of 'black bloc' tactics[92] and no one in the convoy was wearing all black clothing.

The statement by Senator Busson is also full of internal contradictions. For instance, she says that "These occupiers are by definition anarchists." Following that, she then said, "They are professionally led, well-funded, and skilfully planning the downfall of democracy."

To any police officer or a criminal analyst with even the vaguest conception of the anarchist movement in

---

[92] Editors, "Black Bloc," Counter Extremism Project, 2022, https://www.counterextremism.com/supremacy/black-bloc. The Black Bloc refers to a set of dress, tactics, and methodologies employed by anarchist groups. They generally relate to violence with social activist riots as well as vandalism. They mask their identities so they can commit acts of violence and other forms of illegal civil disobedience. The words Black Bloc should be associated to primarily tactics and does not infer that anarchist who employ it are a cohesive movement. **Rated B3.**

Canada, this statement is willfully misleading or functionally stupid.

While it is a separate area of discussion, the anarchist movement in Canada has never been able to generate any momentum or become a systemic threat to national security. They have been responsible for a variety of low-level violent activities at demonstrations such as the G8 or G20 events. They lack cohesive leadership (by definition) and have no funding. Most of them are unemployed or work in low-level service positions.

The View of Anarchists

While difficult to say with precision, real anarchists would probably be insulted at the idea they were running the Freedom Convoy 2022. Anarchist views of the Freedom Convoy were quite negative. An extensive article by Jason Pramas, a self-identified Ottawa anarchist, stated:

> *"There has been fascist, far-right mobilizations in recent years in Ottawa, including an attempt at a similar convoy-style action in 2019... Most of the key organizers and public figures associated with the convoy occupation are involved with a variety of far-right movements... They were ideologically diverse in some ways, but the main currents were right-wing, nationalist, and authoritarian.... The "anti-vaccine mandate" and "anti-lockdown" demands were largely a cover used to further anti-government, right-wing ideologies of personal*

liberty and privilege at the expense of collective care and well-being."[93]

Additionally, it should be noted that the (anarchist) Punch Up Collective made the statement that:

"Although the convoy participants are our enemies, they are just one expression of the far deeper structural and systemic problems we all confront. We desperately need to fight the right in all of the places they're mobilizing. And as we fight the convoys across the country, it's worth asking ourselves how the fights we take on in these specific contexts can build that bigger movement."[94]

Assessment of Anarchism and Freedom Convoy 2022

A variety of possibilities exist as to why a former Commissioner of the RCMP and serving senator in the Government of Canada would make such outlandish and impossible statements. It is possible that Bev Busson became the Commissioner of the RCMP without ever learning about anarchism and the (limited) threat that it poses to Canadian society. It is also possible that she has no idea about how poorly the anarchist felt

---

[93] Jason Pramas, "The Ottawa Freedom Convoy Occupation: A Local Anarchist Perspective," Digboston.com (Dig Media Group Corporation, February 24, 2022), https://digboston.com/the-ottawa-freedom-convoy-occupation-a-local-anarchist-perspective/. **Rated F3.**

[94] Editors, "Organizing against the Occupation of Ottawa," Punch Up Collective, February 6, 2022, https://www.punchupcollective.org/2022/02/06/organizing-against-the-occupation-of-ottawa/. **Rated F3.**

about the entire Freedom Convoy 2022 movement. If so, perhaps her statements can be excused as those of ignorance.

Alternatively, it is possible that the (Trudeau-appointed) Senator felt it necessary to back up the position of the Liberal Government and her statement to the Senate was created in an *evidence-free* manner to do just that.

Whatever the situation with Senator Busson, these statements of hers are representative of a larger problem in Canadian politics. Far-reaching accusations are made without any evidence. They are then entered into the public record to influence Canadians and those with an interest in Canada.

CHAPTER 12: THE ANTI-SEMITISM HOAX

On 6 February 2022, the Chair of the (ironically named) Canadian Anti-Hate Network put out a Tweet showing a photo of a pamphlet that had the title "EVERY SINGLE ASPECT OF THE COVID AGENDA IS JEWISH." This Chairman made the comment "Taken by a friend at the Occupation. Apparently in plain site."

This antisemitic story was immediately seized upon by a variety of reporters and journalists, despite no source being provided or any evidence of its existence in Ottawa.

Among those who picked up on the false material and attempted to make political gains with it were:

- Reporter and Anchor Angie Seth of CTV: "this is both disgusting and horrifying,"[95]
- NDP Member of Parliament Charlie Angus posted: The #ottawaoccupation gang came to Ottawa with swastikas scrawled on Canadian flags," said Angus. "This shit isn't hidden, it's right there in the open."[96]

---

[95] Bernie Farber, "Chair of Trudeau-Funded 'Anti-Hate' Network Spreads Antisemitism Hoax to Smear Canadian Truckers," The Post Millennial | Opinion (The Post Millennial, February 6, 2022), https://thepostmillennial.com/chair-of-trudeau-funded-anti-hate-network-spreads-antisemitic-hoax-to-smear-canadian-truckers. **Rated C2.**
[96] Jonathan Kay, "NDP MP Charlie Angus Fell for It, of Course.," Twitter (Twitter Inc., February 6, 2022), https://twitter.com/jonkay/status/1490444076885422084.

- Erica Ifill of the Hill Times stated: "There is no white supremacy that doesn't start with anti-Semitism and anti-Blackness."[97]
- Joe Cressy, Chair of the Toronto Board of Health: "Don't look away. This vile anti-Semitic hate is being distributed in plain sight. It has no place on the streets of Canadian cities. It has no place anywhere. Call it out, condemn it, don't associate with it, and shut this type of hatred down.[98]
- Kyle Harrietha, Deputy Chief of Staff and Director of Parliamentary Affairs to Canada's Minister of Natural Resources stated: This is sick.

The Real Source of the Photo of the Pamphlet

The alleged photo of the pamphlet found in Ottawa was not taken in Ottawa during the Freedom Convoy 2022 protests.

It was taken in Miami, approximately two weeks earlier. The Cleveland Jewish News published an article on 24 January 2022 showing the same photo of the same flyer, right down to the same wrinkles in the paper and

Not Rated.
[97] Jonathan Kay, "Ottawa Journo," Twitter (Twitter Inc., February 6, 2022),
https://twitter.com/jonkay/status/1490442908671033349.
Not rated.
[98] Jonathan Kay, "Chair of the Toronto Board of Health," Twitter (Twitter Inc., February 6, 2022),
https://twitter.com/jonkay/status/1490444065258811400.
Not rated.

the same background. A side-by-side comparison of the two same photos can be seen online.[99] According to the Cleveland Jewish News article, the flyer had been distributed in Florida neighbourhoods overnight on 22 January 2022. A photo of the flyer was shared by the Twitter account @BecauseMiami on 23 January.[100]

The issue of the photo having been taken much earlier was raised by Jonathon Kay of Quillette. The online conversation between Kay and the Chair of the Canadian Anti-Hate Network went like this:[101]

(Kay) "Wow Bernie, isn't it incredible that the picture your 'friend in Ottawa at the Occupation' sent you is identical to the photo posted on Twitter two weeks ago

[99] Jonathan Kay, "Wow Bernie, Isn't It Incredible That the Picture Your 'Friend in Ottawa at the Occupation' Sent You Is Identical to the Photo Posted on Twitter Two Weeks Ago by Someone in Miami, Right down to the Ceramic Design in the Background?," Twitter (Twitter Inc., February 6, 2022), https://twitter.com/jonkay/status/1490439304224686082. **Not Rated.**

[100] Becky Raspe, "Antisemitic Flyer Distributed in Florida Neighborhoods | National News ...," Cleveland Jewish News (Cleveland Jewish Publication Company, January 24, 2022), https://www.clevelandjewishnews.com/news/national_news /antisemitic-flyer-distributed-in-florida-neighborhoods/article_9bae08e0-7d39-11ec-8710-e763dfe6ca2a.html. **Rated C2.**

[101] The Post Millennial, "Chair of Trudeau-Funded 'Anti-Hate' Network Spreads Antisemitism Hoax to Smear Canadian Truckers," The Post Millennial, February 6, 2022, https://thepostmillennial.com/chair-of-trudeau-funded-anti-hate-network-spreads-antisemitic-hoax-to-smear-canadian-truckers. **Rated C2.**

by someone in Miami, right down to the ceramic design in the background?"

(Chair of CANH) "Jon, respectfully, antisemitic and racist flyers are produced and too easily accessible online to be copied and distributed. This particular flyer is not new to me either."

(Kay) "You told us the image was from the Ottawa Occupation. The photo you tweeted was taken in Miami two weeks ago."

(Chair of CAHN) "Yes in fact that photo has been reproduced numerous times I'm told over the last few weeks." (The Chair seems to contradict his own position here).

(Kay) "But that's not what you said. You posted the photo and said it was from the Ottawa occupation. Instead, it was a photo that someone took in Miami, and then you got it and told everyone it was taken in Ottawa."

(Chair of the CAHN) "The pic sent to me was of a copy of this flyer allegedly seen in Ottawa where the picture I posted was taken. And yes, it's been seen elsewhere as well. Apologies for my unclear language."

Parliamentary Hearing

During parliamentary hearings, the Canadian Anti-Hate Network was questioned by Conservative MP Dane Lloyd about this photo and its origin and why the Chair of the Network made the claim. The Executive Director of the network said that "someone" reached out to them. The Network says they had seen the same flyer in Ottawa. The Network had to admit that they had no evidence other than hearsay that the pamphlet was ever distributed in Ottawa.[102]

The CAHN did not identify who was the "someone" who reached out to them.

The Canadian Anti-Hate Network's Funding

The Canadian Anti-Hate Network received $268,000 in Canadian government funding in 2020. The funding was to "increase the organization's capacity to counter online hate by hiring four team members to carry out the monitoring of extreme-right groups, report on their activities, and file complaints with law enforcement; it will educate the public as to these groups and the damage they create and will share information through its Facebook and Twitter followers."[103]

---

[102] Cosmin Dzsurdzsa, "Conservative MP Dane Lloyd Grilled the Canadian Anti-Hate Network Today for Falsely Claiming That an Anti-Semitic Flyer from Miami, Florida Was at the Freedom Convoy Protest. Executive Director Admits They Didn't Verify the Photo and Relied on Hearsay. (Clip Sped up for Time.)," Twitter (Twitter Inc., April 26, 2022), https://twitter.com/cosmindzs/status/151904668081280204 8. **Not rated**.

[103] Canadian Heritage, "Backgrounder – Building a More Inclusive Canada: Government of Canada Announces Funding for Anti-Racism Projects Across the Country," Canada.ca (Government of Canada, October 26, 2020), https://www.canada.ca/en/canadian-heritage/news/2020/10/backgrounder--building-a-more-inclusive-canada-government-of-canada-announces-funding-for-anti-racism-projects-across-the-country.html. **Not Rated**.

It would appear, at least in this case, that the CAHN has a weak spot in its assessments.

Assessment

No evidence has been produced that the flyer was seen in Canada. The "friend" who took the photo was never identified.

Many politicians and journalists immediately spread this report, lacking any source information or evidence that the supposed event of seeing the pamphlet had even occurred.

It is possible to assess, in the greater context of Canadian politics, that this group of 'journalists' and politicians willfully spread this information as it fits their hate-filled agenda driven by the politics of identity. Each one of these persons should have known better – you should not be reporting information that has no source and appears on social media. "A friend sent me a picture" is not a source.

It is easy to blame the Canadian Anti-Hate Network for this seeming hoax, but the lesson here is that the agenda of many 'progressive' politicians and journalists keep getting exposed. They are so desperate to create wedge issues and divisions in Canadian society that they repeat even false information to push their agendas.

CHAPTER 13: HORSES, BICYCLES AND LIES

On Friday, 18 February 2022 at approximately 5:14 PM, Candice "Candy" Sero, of the Tyendinaga Mohawk Territory was trampled by a Toronto Police Service horse. The incident occurred on the site of the Ottawa Freedom Convoy 2022 protest near the intersection of Rideau Street and Mackenzie Avenue.[104] At the time, a variety of police forces were attempting to move protestors out of the area.

In a video recorded just before she was trampled, she stated that her purpose at the protest was for her children and grandchildren and that she was there for "peace, love and happiness."[105]

A video of the event was taken as it was happening. The videographer can be heard saying, "They just trampled that lady. They just fully trampled that lady."[106]

---

[104] Derek Baldwin, "SIU Probes Reported Injury of Mohawk Woman after Ottawa Incident with Police Horse," The Whig (The Kingston Whig Standard, February 22, 2022), https://www.thewhig.com/news/siu-probes-reported-injury-of-mohawk-woman-in-ottawa-incident-with-police-horse . **Rated B2.**

[105] Alissa Golob, "After This Elderly Woman Explains to the Police That She Is Participating in the Protest for Her Children and Grandchildren and for 'Peace, Love and Happiness', She Gets Trampled by Policemen on Horseback," Twitter (Twitter, February 18, 2022), https://twitter.com/alissagolob/status/1494815873944616960 .

[106] Patricia McKnight, "Video Appears to Show Police Horses Trampling Canadian Trucker Protesters," Newsweek

In responding to this incident, the Ottawa Police statement of 19 February 2022[107] stated that:

"We hear your concern for people on the ground after the horses dispersed a crowd. Anyone who fell got up and walked away. We're unaware of any injuries. A bicycle was thrown at the horse further down the line and caused the horse to trip. The horse was uninjured."

Candy Sero was protesting legally. First Nations Canadians were not subject to the Emergency Act that had been put into place as of 14 February 2022. According to government regulations put out after the declaration of the Emergencies Act, the powers do not apply to (a) a person registered as an Indian under the Indian Act; (b) a person who has been recognized as a Convention refugee.[108] It is not clear from the

---

(Newsweek Digital LLC, February 22, 2022), https://www.newsweek.com/video-appears-show-police-horses-trampling-canadian-trucker-protesters-1680847. **Rated B3.**

[107] Ottawa Police, "We Hear Your Concern for People on the Ground after the Horses Dispersed a Crowd. Anyone Who Fell Got up and Walked Away. We're Unaware of Any Injuries. A Bicycle Was Thrown at the Horse Further down the Line and Caused the Horse to Trip. The Horse Was Uninjured.," Twitter (Twitter, February 19, 2022), https://twitter.com/OttawaPolice/status/1495026664845328388.

[108] Brian Lilley, "Emergencies Act Regulations Ban Protests except for Indigenous or Refugees," Toronto Sun (Postmedia Network Inc., February 18, 2022), https://torontosun.com/news/national/emergencies-act-regulations-ban-protests-except-for-indigenous-or-refugees.

regulations why First Nations or refugees are not covered by the Emergencies Act.

When Newsweek Magazine contacted the Ottawa Police for a comment, the spokesperson said that "no protestors were trampled…. "We understand that one protestor fell, got up, and walked away."[109] (Of note, the police horse in question belongs to the Toronto Police Service and not the Ottawa Police.)

Like so many other narratives deriving from the Freedom Convoy, the Ottawa Police statement is willfully misleading. Candy Sero did not fall, contrary to the statement. She was trampled by a horse as was another person directly in front of her.

Additionally, leaked texts from police showed they thought the trampling of the person in question was funny. One police person, identified as "Marca" stated:

> *"just watched the horse video – that is awesome"*
> *"we should practice that maneuver"*[110]

Concerning the brutality, RCMP Musical Ride member, Andrew Nixon stated that:

---

[109] Patricia McKnight, "Video Appears to Show Police Horses Trampling Canadian Trucker Protesters," Newsweek (Newsweek Digital LLC, February 22, 2022) **Rated B3.**
[110] Sheila Gunn Reid, "LEAKED RCMP MESSAGES: 'Time for the Protesters to Hear Our Jackboots on the Ground,'" Rebel News (Rebel News Network Ltd., February 19, 2022), https://www.rebelnews.com/leaked_rcmp_messages_time_f or_the_protesters_to_hear_our_jackboots_on_the_ground. **Rated C3.**

"Time for the protesters to hear our jackboots on the ground"[111]

The comments seem to support the idea that not only were the rank-and-file police members aware that the public statements about the horse trampling event were not correct. They seem aware that their personnel did trample Candy Sero and they found it rather amusing.

Fall Out

Following the Freedom Convoy, the Canadian Prime Minister was on a European visit in March 2022. It was related to the war in Ukraine. He referred to "peace and security" and "defending democracy" concerning the Russian invasion of Ukraine. A variety of Members of the European Parliament (MEP) walked out of his speech. Some suggested he was a "disgrace to democracy" while an MEP from Croatia[112] referred to the Canadian Prime Minister and stated:

---

[111] Royal Canadian Mounted Police, "Statement on Material Circulating on Social Media Regarding Some RCMP Members," Blockades News (Royal Canadian Mounted Police, February 20, 2022), https://blockade.rcmp.ca/news-nouvelles/ncr-rcn201500-s-d-en.html. The RCMP appeared to confirm the authenticity of the texts when they put out a formal statement on the matter. While acknowledging the material in the texts, they stated they were looking into the matter. **Rated A1.**

[112] The Croatian MEP's statement is on his Twitter feed at https://twitter.com/unhealthytruth/status/1506910780767285249

"Unfortunately, today there are those among us who trample on these fundament values. Canada, once a symbol of the modern world, has become a symbol of civil rights violations under your quasi-liberal boot in recent months. We have watched as you trample women with horses... To you, there may be liberal methods, for many citizens of the world, it is a dictatorship of the worst kind."[113] (Emphasis added.)

Assessment

The official statement by the Ottawa Police which tried to suggest that Candy Sero was somehow responsible for her trampling is typical of the entire government narrative. While the horse trampled the victim in question (plus at least one other person), the police attempted to transfer blame to Freedom Convoy protestors. The statement that someone threw a bicycle is incorrect and no bicycle appears in the drone footage or any other videos at the time.

---

[113] Mislav Kolakusic MEP, "PM Trudeau, in Recent Months, under Your Quasi-Liberal Boot, Canada Has Become a Symbol of Civil Rights Violations. The Methods We Have Witnessed May Be Liberal to You, but to Many Citizens around the World It Seemed like a Dictatorship of the Worst Kind.," Twitter (Twitter, March 23, 2022), https://twitter.com/mislavkolakusic/status/15067024852259 38949. Video of the full statement by the Croatian Member of the European Parliament. **Rated A1.**

CHAPTER 14: ECONOMIC DAMAGE

One of the key drivers for the Emergencies Act at the federal level and the Ontario provincial Emergency Measures Act was alleged to be economic damage from border blockades. Neither of the two border crossing protests (Ontario, Alberta) was started or controlled by Freedom Convoy 2022. They were independent actions created by the spontaneous support for the protest in Ottawa.

Nonetheless, these two activities were put forth as one of the key reasons for the national level Emergencies Act. Ironically, both protests had been dispersed before the Emergencies Act was declared.

Among the various statements and headlines concerning the economic damage of the border protests were:

- *Convoy protests disrupt auto industry on US-Canada border.*[114]
- *Trudeau: Convoy blockade causing 'real harm' on both sides of the border*[115]

---

[114] Caroline Vakil, "Convoy Protests Disrupt Auto Industry on US-Canada Border," The Hill (NEXSTAR Inc., February 10, 2022), https://thehill.com/policy/transportation/593698-convoy-protests-disrupt-auto-industry-on-us-canada-border/. **Rated C3.**

[115] Lexi Lonas, "Trudeau: Convoy Blockade Causing 'Real Harm' on Both Sides of the Border," The Hill (NEXSTAR Inc., February 11, 2022), https://thehill.com/policy/international/593867-trudeau-

- *Public Safety Minister Marco Mendicino said the government had no choice because the closure of U.S. border crossings and downtown Ottawa was damaging the economy.[116]*
- *Ambassador Bridge blockade stalled billions in trade — and there could be other effects: expert[117]*
- *As the blockades have shown, anarchy is usually bad for business[118]*
- Premier Ford of Ontario says he will "*urgently enact orders that will make crystal clear it is illegal and punishable to block and impede the movement of goods, people and services along with critical infrastructure.*"[119]

convoy-blockade-causing-real-harm-on-both-sides-of-the-border/. **Rated C3.**

[116] Ryan Tumilty, "Government Had No Choice but to Invoke Emergencies Act, Liberal Ministers Tell Committee," Windsor Star (Postmedia Network Inc., April 26, 2022), https://windsorstar.com/news/politics/government-had-no-choice-but-to-invoke-emergencies-act-public-safety-minister-tells-commons-committee. **Rated C4.**

[117] Jennifer La Grassa, "Ambassador Bridge Blockade Stalled Billions in Trade - and There Could Be Other Effects: Expert," CBC News Windsor (CBC/Radio Canada, February 15, 2022), https://www.cbc.ca/news/canada/windsor/ambassador-bridge-protest-cost-1.6351312. **Rated C4.**

[118] Don Pittis, "As the Blockades Have Shown, Anarchy Is Usually Bad for Business," CBC News Business - Analysis (CBC/Radio Canada, February 15, 2022), https://www.cbc.ca/news/business/anarchism-convoy-column-don-pittis-1.6347821. **Rated C4.**

[119] Gabby Rodrigues, "Premier Doug Ford Declares State of Emergency amid Protests at Land Border and in Ottawa," Global News Canada (Global News, a division of Corus

Economic Report

The claims by the Government of Canada that the blockades were causing economic damage turned out to be false. Despite all the claims of damage, it turns out that cross-border trade for both Alberta and Ontario was up about 16% from the same period one year previous.

Martin Jansen, who is the general manager of the Fort Macleod-based seed processor Arjazon stated that: "The first couple days we basically came to a halt." But once CBSA began redirecting traffic to other crossings, the problems ended. He continues, "Once it was open it worked out well. The first week was pretty bad, but after that, we found other routes and we just kept going."

While concerns were expressed about the vegetable trade which has short shelf lives, the US vegetable trade was up seven percent in Ontario, and 66 percent in Alberta compared to the previous year, according to data from StatCan.[120]

Entertainment Inc., February 11, 2022), https://globalnews.ca/news/8612348/ontario-doug-ford-border-protests-announcement/. **Rated B3**.

[120] Max Hartshorn, *The economic nightmare that wasn't? Border blockades had little effect on trade, data reveals,* 26 April 2022, Global News. The article can be seen online at https://www.msn.com/en-ca/news/other/the-economic-nightmare-that-wasn-t-border-blockades-had-little-effect-on-trade-data-reveals/ar-AAWBhgi?ocid=msedgntp&cvid=07f73bf1a3374a5688315fcd816c3f6e. **Rated C2**.

A differing assessment can be made for the automotive trade. While claims were made by the Government of Canada about protest-induced losses, other observers were less clear. "Analyst Peter Nagle, of the automotive research firm S&P Global Mobility, notes that cross-border trade in completed vehicles was down this January and February compared to last year. However, he believes this decline is a result of global supply chain issues that have bedeviled automakers. "Supply chain shortages have limited overall production across the North American light vehicle industry."[121]

Assessment

According to Public Safety Minister Marco Mendicino, "We lost about $390 million a day in trade. Plants were closed, workers were laid off and the manufacturing sector was stalled."[122] The same statement was made

---

[121] Max Hartshorn, "The Economic Nightmare That Wasn't? Border Blockades Had Little Effect on Trade, Data Reveals," Global News (MSN.com, April 26, 2022), https://www.msn.com/en-ca/news/other/the-economic-nightmare-that-wasn-t-border-blockades-had-little-effect-on-trade-data-reveals/ar-AAWBhgi?ocid=msedgntp&cvid=07f73bf1a3374a5688315fcd816c3f6e. **Rated C2.**

[122] Ryan Tumilty, *Government had no choice but to invoke Emergencies Act, Liberal ministers tell committee,* 26 April 2022, Windsor Star. The article can be seen online at https://windsorstar.com/news/politics/government-had-no-choice-but-to-invoke-emergencies-act-public-safety-minister-tells-commons-committee . **Rated C4.**

by Deputy Prime Minister and Finance Minister Chrystia Freeland.[123]

These statements are false. It may be fair to say that trade was affected – that is to say shipping routes were changed. But a variety of politicians and other observers have attempted to infer that these were losses, when in fact they were not.

As noted above, trade in the two provinces affected (Ontario and Alberta) increased for the month involved.

Ottawa Business

While it is somewhat of a separate issue, it is also worthy of note that City of Ottawa officials as well as the CBC[124] claimed that businesses in Ottawa lost up to $200 million due to the Freedom Convoy 2022. A federal relief program was established for businesses claiming hardship during twenty-three days of shutdowns. Grants of $10,000 to $15,000 were made available. The federal program was allocated $20

---

[123] Max Hartshorn, *The economic nightmare that wasn't? Border blockades had little effect on trade, data reveals,* 26 April 2022, Global News. The article can be seen online at https://www.msn.com/en-ca/news/other/the-economic-nightmare-that-wasn-t-border-blockades-had-little-effect-on-trade-data-reveals/ar-AAWBhgi?ocid=msedgntp&cvid=07f73bf1a3374a5688315fcd816c3f6e . **Rated C2**.
[124] Priscilla Ki Sun Hwang, "'Freedom Convoy' Cost Downtown Ottawa Millions per Day, Experts Estimate," CBC News Ottawa (CBC/Radio Canada, March 11, 2022), https://www.cbc.ca/news/canada/ottawa/economic-impact-freedom-convoy-downtown-ottawa-1.6376248. **Rated C4**.

million. According to the CEO of the agency administering the program, it was about 37% undersubscribed as far fewer than expected businesses had applied.[125]

Missing from the Ottawa figures are the number of businesses that made large sales due to the presence of the Freedom Convoy 2022. Several restaurants and convenience stores in the downtown core remained open despite pressure to close from the city. On occasion, they had customers lined up outside the doors. No press report can be found on those companies that prospered because of the convoy, presumably because of the mainstream media narrative that would not allow such reporting.

---

[125] Editors, "Crisis Fund Under Subscribed," Blacklock's Reporter (1395804 Ontario Ltd, April 18, 2022), https://www.blacklocks.ca/crisis-fund-under-subscribed/. **Rated B2.**

CHAPTER 15: THE WAR MEMORIAL

One of the most vitriolic political and media campaigns against Freedom Convoy 2022 was that surrounding the alleged "desecration" of the National War Memorial. The manufactured outrage had both a domestic and international aspect.

Among the headlines were:

- Police launch investigation after member of Canada trucker convoy filmed dancing on tomb of unknown soldier[126];
- Top Canadian defence officials condemn protesters dancing on Tomb of the Unknown Soldier[127];
- Anti-vaxxers danced on Tomb of the Unknown Soldier and desecrated National War Memorial[128];

---

[126] Arpan Rai, "Police Launch Investigation after Member of Canada Trucker Convoy Filmed Dancing on Tomb of Unknown Soldier," The Independent (Independent Digital News and Media Ltd, January 31, 2022), https://www.independent.co.uk/news/world/americas/otta wa-protests-trucker-freedom-convoy-soldier-tomb-b2004298.html. **Rated D3.**

[127] Josh Pringle, "Top Canadian Defence Officials Condemn Protesters Dancing on Tomb of the Unknown Soldier," CTV New Ottawa (Bell Media, January 30, 2022), https://ottawa.ctvnews.ca/top-canadian-defence-officials-condemn-protesters-dancing-on-tomb-of-the-unknown-soldier-1.5760168. **Rated D3.**

[128] Nicole Thompson, "Anti-Vaxxers Danced on Tomb of the Unknown Soldier and Desecrated National War Memorial," Canada's National Observer (Observer Media Group, January

- Police look to identify suspect in desecration of the Tomb of the Unknown Soldier.129

The comments from a variety of officials towards the "protestors" were equally venomous. Among them were:

- Erin O'Toole (then) Leader of the Conservative Party - The individuals desecrating these memorials should be ashamed and their behaviour undermines the brave Canadians who have sacrificed for our country.130
- Chief of Defence Staff General Eyre - "I am sickened to see protesters dance on the Tomb of the Unknown Soldier and desecrate the National War Memorial."131,[132]

29, 2022), https://www.nationalobserver.com/2022/01/29/news/anti-vaxxers-danced-tomb-unknown-soldier-and-desecrated-national-war-memorial. **Rated D3**.

[129] Josh Pringle, "Police Look to Identify Suspect in Desecration of the Tomb of the Unknown Soldier," CTV News Ottawa (Bell Media, February 2, 2022), https://ottawa.ctvnews.ca/police-look-to-identify-suspect-in-desecration-of-the-tomb-of-the-unknown-soldier-1.5765615. **Rated C3**.

[130] Erin O'Toole, "The Individuals Desecrating These Memorials Should Be Ashamed and Their Behaviour Undermines the Brave Canadians Who Have Sacrificed for Our Country.," Twitter (Twitter Inc., January 29, 2022), https://twitter.com/erinotoole/status/148758962449535795 5. **Not Rated**.

[131] Josh Pringle, "Police Look to Identify Suspect in Desecration of the Tomb of the Unknown Soldier," CTV News Ottawa (Bell Media, February 2, 2022). **Rated C3**.

- NDP Leader Jagmeet Singh - "Claiming to be fighting for freedom while disrespecting those who lost their lives fighting for our freedom is despicable."133
- Minister of Defence Anita Anand – "beyond reprehensible."134

The Investigational Outcomes

An investigation into the incident of the woman dancing on the Tomb of the Unknown Soldier revealed that this person had no connection to the Freedom Convoy 2022. She was not charged with any offence. Her name was not released. According to a police statement:

> *"She was spoken to, showed remorse for her actions and police are confident she will not re-offend. She*

---

132 General / Général Wayne Eyre, "I Am Sickened to See Protesters Dance on the Tomb of the Unknown Soldier and Desecrate the National War Memorial. Generations of Canadians Have Fought and Died for Our Rights, Including Free Speech, but Not This. Those Involved Should Hang Their Heads in Shame.," Twitter (Twitter Inc., January 29, 2022), https://twitter.com/CDS_Canada_CEMD/status/1487555335 627943938. **Not Rated.**

133 Hannah Jackson, "'Several' Investigations Underway after Monuments Defaced during Ottawa Trucker Rally: Police," Global News (Global News, a division of Corus Entertainment Inc. Corus News., January 31, 2022), https://globalnews.ca/news/8581382/ottawa-police-investigations-trucker-rally/. **Rated D3.**

134 Josh Pringle, "Police Look to Identify Suspect in Desecration of the Tomb of the Unknown Soldier," CTV News Ottawa (Bell Media, February 2, 2022) **Rated C3.**

was processed by other means, which is a police practice."[135]

Assessment

The false story around a Freedom Convoy 2022 participant desecrating the National War Memorial appears to be a case of deliberately generated fake outrage. The situation was complicated by a series of senior officials and reporters making evidence-free accusations.

Given the public outrage about the event, it does seem strange that the person will not be charged because she "showed remorse." It can be questioned as to whether the person would have been charged if they were shown to have had an affiliation with the Freedom Convoy.

---

[135] Michael Woods, "Woman Who Stood on Tomb of the Unknown Soldier Won't Be Charged: Police," CTV News Ottawa (Bell Media, April 28, 2022), https://ottawa.ctvnews.ca/woman-who-stood-on-tomb-of-the-unknown-soldier-won-t-be-charged-police-1.5880365. **Rated C3.**

CHAPTER 16: FREEZING ACCOUNTS TESTIMONY

During testimony to the House Finance Committee (FINA) on 7 March 2022, RCMP Assistant Commissioner Michel Arcand stated that protestors had been warned before their bank and other financial accounts were frozen. He also stated that at least 257 accounts belonging to 57 different entities were frozen. (The use of the term 'entity' here refers to the fact that some commercial accounts belonging to media organizations were frozen.) Arcand also states that the action was directed at key protest figures to "discourage the people that are influencing the protests."[136] (Emphasis added)

RCMP Superintendent Denis Beaudoin, director of the RCMP's financial crimes division stated: "We contacted [protesters] before providing information to financial institutions."

Assessment

Questions were put to a variety of individuals who could be identified as key figures in the protest. Of the individuals who had a variety of bank, credit card, and

---

[136] Noé Chartier, "RCMP Say Freezing Convoy Protesters' Accounts Necessary as Opposition MPs Question Why Court Orders Not Used," www.theepochtimes.com (The Epoch Times, March 9, 2022), https://www.theepochtimes.com/rcmp-say-freezing-convoy-protesters-accounts-necessary-as-opposition-mps-question-why-court-orders-not-used_4323166.html. **Rated B3.**

payment accounts closed, none of them reported having received any warning calls from any officials on this matter.

A number of those persons had been in contact with police and civic officials throughout the protest timeframe, so their mobile phone numbers were known to the police. Several other persons involved were former police or intelligence personnel, so their names, addresses, and phone numbers would have been easy to determine.

In this case, the parliamentary evidence given to House Finance Committee (FINA) by an RCMP Assistant Commissioner, and a Superintendent cannot be matched with inquiries to those affected. Again, this appears to be another case of false testimony by government officials to Parliament and to Canadian citizens.

CHAPTER 17: THE DOCTOR'S EVENT

While Freedom Convoy 2022 held several public events from prayer services to street dances, among the most popular figures were "The Doctors." It is rare to hear doctors described as 'rock stars' but such was the case with their live events and videos.

Much of the discontent that drove tens of thousands of people to attend Freedom Convoy events was driven by the arbitrary lockdowns and vaccine mandates. These mandates and forced vaccine programs[137] were without a scientific basis. Further to that, all the work on preparing for pandemics ahead of time done by Emergency Measures Organizations focused on brief lockdowns only and voluntary vaccine programs.

The purpose of the Freedom Convoy doctor's press conference was to invite senior officials from the federal government to make a presentation and show the scientific evidence they were using to justify the lockdowns and the variety of punitive measures such as the trucking mandates.

---

[137] The issue of whether vaccines were 'forced' on Canadians can be seen as contentious. However, the reality is that you could be fired from your job, lose your house, be publicly attacked by the government, have your children exposed to ridicule if you/they were not vaccinated. Children were publicly shamed and blocked from school and sporting programs if they were not jabbed. While some government officials have attempted to say no one was 'forced' to take a vaccine, the reality remains that the government's approach was highly coercive.

The government officials were invited personally and through the Prime Minister's Office at the same time. Follow-up was done to ensure they had received the invites.

The Event

On 11 February 2022, Freedom Convoy 2022 held the "Doctors' Press Conference" which was more formally called a Public Scientific Forum.

Those doctors presenting on the behalf of Freedom Convoy 2022 were Dr. Byram Bridle, Dr. Paul Alexander, and Dr. Roger Hodkinson. The moderator for the event was Dr. Laura Braeden.

Those invited to the forum to represent the Government of Canada were Dr. Theresa Tam and Dr. Howard Njoo and the Chair of the National Advisory Committee on Immunization, Dr. Shelley Deeks.[138]

The Government of Canada failed to respond to the invitations and none of the invitees were present.

As an aside, the mainstream media, which constantly complained about not having access to the Freedom Convoy was also invited. Not a single representative from the mainstream media attended.

---

[138] Dr. Byram W. Bridle, "Doctors Supporting the Freedom Convoy 2022 to Convene Public Scientific Forum," Doctors Supporting the Freedom Convoy 2022 to Convene Public Scientific Forum (COVID Chronicles, February 7, 2022), https://viralimmunologist.substack.com/p/doctors-supporting-the-freedom-convoy?s=r. **Rated B2.**

Assessment

The Government of Canada had a perfect opportunity to present scientific information to back its decision to impose stricter mandates on the trucking industry. They also could have used the platform to present information backing their program of forced vaccinations.

If the Government of Canada has been able to present even one scientific paper backing up their decision-making process, it would have completely undermined Freedom Convoy 2022 and its challenge to arbitrary rule making.

They chose to not show up.

Putting their activity (or lack thereof) in context, it is fair to say as they failed to attend as they had no credible evidence to present.[139]

As with many other aspects of mandates and lockdowns, they were more intended to be coercive measures to punish those who did not submit to the program of vaccinating the population with an experimental sleight of vaccines.

The failure of the mainstream media to attend added to the belief that the media will only report on government-friendly events that support whatever

---

[139] In the Federal Court, the refusal to answer a question can be interpreted by the judge as indicative of guilt. By analogy, the same standard can be applied here. A failure to provide an answer is indicative of the absence of evidence.

narrative the government is advocating at that time. While the mainstream media complains about this situation, this would appear to be another case where they helped destroy their credibility.

CHAPTER 18: HUMAN SLIME

On the 17th of February 2022, Fareed Khan of *Canadians United Against Hate* addressed himself to Conservative Party Member of Parliament and interim leader Candice Bergen on Twitter. The tweet read:

> *"And you and the Conservatives had an opportunity not to side with #fascists, #NeoNazis, #racists, #WhiteSumpremacists, #Islamophobes and #AntiSemites. If you want to associate with <u>human slime</u> don't be surprised if that label gets attached to you. @theJagmeetSingh @JustinTrudeau"* (Emphasis added)[140]

The day before that, Fareed Khan had also stated that:

> *"ANY Conservative MPs who support #FluTrucksKlan protestors or call for more demonstrations are violating police order and need to be arrested under Sections 51 and 59 of the Criminal Code. #FluTruxKlanGoHome."*[141]

---

[140] Cosmin Dzsurdzsa, "Journalist Was Tom Korski from @Mindingottawa. These Are the Tweets Canadians United against Hate's Fareed Khan Denied during the Press Conference. Pic.twitter.com/0mcrhg4epz," Twitter (Google LLC, April 14, 2022), https://twitter.com/cosminDZS/status/1514780960134377479. **Not Rated**.
[141] Cosmin Dzsurdzsa, "Journalist Was Tom Korski from @Mindingottawa. These Are the Tweets Canadians United against Hate's Fareed Khan Denied during the Press Conference. Pic.twitter.com/0mcrhg4epz," Twitter (Google LLC, April 14, 2022). **Not Rated.**

Additionally, Fareed Khan has called for public employees to be fired if they donated to the Freedom Convoy 2022. He stated:

"Any publicly funded employee whether civil servant, police, military personnel or health care worker who funded the insurrection and supported sedition needs to be removed from their job."[142]

In April at an Ottawa Conference marking the 40th Anniversary of the Charter of Rights, Blacklock's Reporter Tom Korski asked why no one from the panels had discussed the Government of Canada's implementation of the Emergencies Act. Mr. Korski then followed up and addressed Fareed Khan directly. He stated:

"That seems an odd omission for this panel. And I wondered why, Mr. Khan – I looked up your social media accounts – you described Freedom Convoy protesters as 'human slime,' – I'm quoting. You said that plaintiffs awaiting bail hearings charged with mischief 'deserve to spend years in jail. You said any publicly funded employee including a nurse who donated a penny to the Freedom Convoy needs to be removed from their job. That was on February 16 – on your Twitter account – and you said any Conservative MP who supported protesters needs to be arrested. Mr. Khan, that's a little bit rough

---

[142] Editors, "Read Your Charter, Feds Told," Blacklock's Reporter, April 18, 2022, https://www.blacklocks.ca/read-your-charter-feds-told/. **Rated B2.**

coming from an advocate of the Charter of Rights and Freedoms."[143]

Mr. Khan responded by saying that he did not remember using the term 'human slime'. He then added that:

"This was a protest organized by people with a known history of racism and white supremacy, Islamophobia, anti-semitism. They allowed white supremacists and neo-Nazis to march around freely within the protests; they had no problem with that. And frankly, the politicians who stood by these protest organizers and enabled them – encouraged them, in my view – were committing sedition under the Criminal Code."

Mr. Khan did not provide any evidence for his statements, nor did he elaborate on any sources or information for this statement. [144]

Assessment

Fareed Khan, according to his Carleton University website entry, has a "knack for articulate message development and delivery allows him to address

---

[143] Harley Sims, "Government Charter of Rights Conference Concludes with Sharp Words for Panelists," True North (True North Centre for Public Policy, April 19, 2022), https://tnc.news/2022/04/19/government-charter-of-rights-conference-concludes-with-sharp-words-for-panelists/. **Rated B2.**

[144] Harley Sims, "Government Charter of Rights Conference Concludes with Sharp Words for Panelists," True North (True North Centre for Public Policy, April 19, 2022). **Rated B2.**

complex issues, and forge networks of influential contacts at the local, provincial, and federal government levels."[145]

As someone who professes to favour equality and human rights, it would seem unusual to refer to a female Member of Parliament as being worthy of the label "human slime."

Anti-Hate Groups

Aside from this statement, it seems curious that a variety of "anti-hate" organizations which are funded or have sought funding from the Government of Canada use the most hateful terms in public discourse.

While there is not sufficient evidence to make a clear statement, it does seem – in context – that groups that have both an "anti-hate" mandate and are funded by the Government of Canada or work closely with it do use extreme language. The use of this language, often unsupported by evidence, appears likely to cause more societal divisions or well – ...hatred.

---

[145] Fareed W. Khan, "Fareed Khan: Curriculum Vitae," Academia.edu, September 10, 2021, https://carleton-ca.academia.edu/FareedKhan/CurriculumVitae. **Not Rated**.

CHAPTER 19: CBC AND THE FAKE FINANCIAL STORIES

Unaccounted Donations

On 7 April 2022, the CBC ran an article with the headline *"Almost $8M of 'Freedom Convoy' donations still unaccounted for, documents show."*[146]

The article makes several false or misleading statements to suggest to the reader that donations money remains missing. The subheading reads *"Some money raised sits in escrow, some was returned to donors or spent, and some is unaccounted for."*

The most important claim from the CBC is that the $7.5 million from GiveSendGo is "unaccounted for."

The CBC made this statement even though court documents and GiveSendGo explained where the money went. Approximately half of the money was returned to donors and the other half is in an escrow account.[147] The money is neither missing nor unaccounted for.

---

[146] David Fraser, "Almost $8m of 'Freedom Convoy' Donations Still Unaccounted for, Documents Show | CBC News," CBC News Ottawa (CBC/Radio Canada, April 7, 2022), https://www.cbc.ca/news/canada/ottawa/freedom-convoy-donations-1.6410105. **Rated C4**.

[147] Wyatt Claypool, "Media Lies: The CBC Wrongly Claims $8 Million Went Missing from Freedom Convoy," The National Telegraph, April 9, 2022, https://thenationaltelegraph.com/culture/media-lies-the-cbc-wrongly-claims-8-million-went-missing-from-freedom-

The Donor Story

On the 24th of March 2022, the CBC ran a story with the headline *"I regret going: Protester says he spent life savings to support Freedom Convoy."* The sub-headline reads *"No 'stance' on vaccine mandates, but used own money to help protesters, man says."*

The essence of the story is that Martin Joseph Anglehart lost $13,000 of his own money, lost his home and vehicle, and is now living in an SUV. He is homeless. He now says he regrets being involved in the convoy as it cost him everything and he has "nothing left" after spending his life savings on gas and food for the convoy.[148] Anglehart admits he never had "a stance on mandates" but felt drawn to the movement after he was prevented from visiting a dying friend at a Montreal hospital in June 2020 because of COVID-19 restrictions.

What is missing from the CBC is the following:[149]

- The bank documents the CBC said it viewed as part of the story also reveal Anglehart was

---

convoy. **Rated C3.**

[148] Rachelle Elsiufi, "'I Regret Going': Protester Says He Spent Life Savings to Support Freedom Convoy | CBC News," CBC News Ottawa (CBC/Radio Canada, March 27, 2022), https://www.cbc.ca/news/canada/ottawa/ottawa-convoy-protest-regrets-1.6394502. **Rated D4.**

[149] Angelo Isidorou, "CBC's 'Regretful' Trucker Convoy Protester Story Falls Apart," The Post Millennial (The Post Millennial, March 27, 2022), https://thepostmillennial.com/cbcs-regretful-trucker-convoy-protester-story. **Rated B3.**

receiving welfare from separate provinces, which is fraud.

- Anglehart "scammed many with his false stories of being ex-forces with PTSD and terminal cancer and was robbed. Many gave him money, bought him a new laptop and a bus ticket to an Ottawa treatment facility, and set up a GoFundMe."
- Information collected around Anglehart suggests that he scammed numerous individuals out of thousand of dollars during the protests.
- The bank documents CBC says they checked did not show where the money was going. CBC simply accepted his word for it.
- Anglehart says his bank account was frozen, but there is no information to support this claim and he was never an organizer or supporter.
- The CBC says he was arrested, but there is no evidence for this. He did receive a ticket during the protest, but this is not evidence of an arrest.

The CBC story is sloppy at best and willfully misleading at worst. Perhaps the best that can be said about it is the following, as noted by the Post Millennial in their story:

> "It would appear as though Anglehart is a man with mental health challenges who has been used as a prop by the CBC."

Assessment of the Two CBC Stories

The CBC stories were published on 24 March and 7 April 2022. As such, the CBC cannot claim that the 'fog of war" and the need to publish in the middle of the crisis were a problem.

The stories were written with the fullness of time. There was no deadline pressure.

As with many other CBC stories around Freedom Convoy, they attempted to cast the protest in the worst possible light. As has been shown with other CBC stores that they had to recant, the stories contain information that is false or misleading.

CBC can have no excuse for this. They are heavily funded and have a massive infrastructure of well-paid staff and editors.

The context of CBC's overall history is one of failure in this area. It can be stated with some confidence that the CBC provides biased and misleading report that supports their primary funder – the Government of Canada.

As a side note, it can be said that the CBC is effectively unaccountable to the citizens. While the CBC could be sued for liable in many cases, they have deep pockets and a seemingly endless budget with continuing increases. Even winning a substantial judgment against them would be meaningless as their staff is not accountable, and they would not suffer financially. The bill, as always, would be paid by the taxpayer.

CHAPTER 20: PREMIER FORD OF ONTARIO – A CRIMINAL MIND

The primary purpose of this book is to focus on the role of the federal government and the media of Canada concerning the popular protests of January and February 2022.

It would be remiss, however, to completely ignore the role of the Premier Doug Ford of Ontario. The actions of the Ontario provincial government are worthy of a larger examination than can be carried out here.

The actions of Premier Ford are arguably as bad, or perhaps worse than those of Prime Minister Trudeau. His responses to the protests are indicative of a criminal mind at work.

Premier Ford is, by trade, a hashish dealer. While he and his supporters focus on the family printing business started by his father, Doug Ford's first regular employment of about seven years was spent as a successful drug dealer in the 1980s. His brother Randy was also involved in the drug trade and was once charged with a drug-related kidnapping. The sister of Doug Ford, Kathy, has been the victim of drug-related gun violence.[150] She was shot in the face in an incident that resulted in one person pleading guilty to a gun possession charge and her former boyfriend was shot

---

[150] Greg McArthur and Shannon Kari, "Globe Investigation: The Ford Family's History with Drug Dealing," The Globe and Mail (The Globe and Mail Inc., May 25, 2013), https://www.theglobeandmail.com/news/toronto/globe-investigation-the-ford-familys-history-with-drug-dealing/article12153014/. **Rated B2.**

and killed by her ex-husband, a drug dealer. The ex-boyfriend/murder victim was Michael Kiklas who, along with Kathy Ford, has an association with the Klu Klux Klan and Wolfgang Droege.[151]

Gavin Tighe, a lawyer working for Doug Ford, says the allegations are false. In response to a Global and Mail investigation, he stated that: "Your references to unnamed alleged sources of information represent the height of irresponsible and unprofessional journalism given the gravely serious and specious allegations of substantial criminal conduct."

Of note, Doug Ford did not sue the Globe and Mail for defamation for the article.

On 11 February 2022, Premier Ford declared a provincial state of emergency, stating that "We are now two weeks into the siege of the City of Ottawa. I call it a siege because that is what it is. It's an illegal occupation."[152] There was, of course, no siege in Ottawa. Personnel and vehicles were able to move throughout almost all of the City of Ottawa except for Wellington Street and some two blocks south. The protest was legal according to court rulings

---

[151] Unless otherwise noted, the references to the Ford family and drug dealing derived from the Globe and Mail story noted above.

[152] Katherine DeClerq, "Ontario Declares a State of Emergency to End 'Siege' in Ottawa and Windsor," CTV News Toronto (Bell Media, February 11, 2022), https://toronto.ctvnews.ca/ontario-premier-doug-ford-declares-state-of-emergency-in-effort-to-end-truck-convoy-blockade-1.5777336. **Rated B3.**

One of the most heinous aspects of his actions was the use of Section 490.8 of the Criminal Code. As the Premier put it in a statement:

> *"This section prohibits any person from disposing of, or otherwise dealing with, in any manner whatsoever, any and all monetary donations made through the Freedom Convoy 2022 and the Adopt-a-Trucker campaign pages on the GiveSendGo online fund-raising platform."*[153]

This decision was stunning, although it did not get as much press coverage as the federal emergency act which would follow three days later. By putting this legal mechanism into effect, Premier Ford criminalized the behaviour of anyone who had donated to the (legal) Freedom Convoy through GiveSendGo.

Bill 100 – Keeping Ontario Open Act

The Government of Ontario, under Premier Ford, gave itself extraordinary power by declaring the provincial emergency act. Following that, the Conservative Party of Premier Ford passed Bill 100 with the misleading name of "Keeping Ontario Open Act." The reality is that this is essentially an extension of the emergency act and will allow the province/police to exercise arbitrary powers. Under this new act, the new measures include:

---

[153] Lucas Casaletto, "Ontario Court Freezes Access to Donations for Anti-Mandate Protest from 'GiveSendGo'," CityNews Ottawa (Rogers Sports & Media, February 10, 2022), https://ottawa.citynews.ca/local-news/ontario-court-freezes-access-to-donations-for-anti-mandate-protest-from-givesendgo-5051525. **Rated B3**

- Fines and/or jail time for anyone deemed to be "impeding access to or egress from, or the ordinary use of, protected transportation infrastructure."

- Giving the Registrar of Motor Vehicles the power to suspend or cancel the plate portion of a permit for a commercial motor vehicle or trailer or a CVOR certificate without a hearing.

- Giving police new powers to arrest without a warrant.[154],[155]

Assessment

Ontario – the most populous and economically important province – now has a two-term premier who spent seven years of his life as a hashish dealer. This by itself speaks volumes about politics in Canada. The Conservative Party of Ontario is aware of this and has done nothing.

Did the criminal mindset of Premier Ford play a role in his response to the border protests in Windsor and the Freedom Convoy in Ottawa?

---

[154] Moya Teklu, Cara Zwibel, and Fred Hahn, "Bill 100 Looking to Silence Government Critics," The Standard (Metroland Media Group Ltd., April 12, 2022), https://www.stcatharinesstandard.ca/opinion/contributors/2022/04/12/bill-100-looking-to-silence-government-critics.html.

[155] Antonella Artuso, "Ford Seeks Emergency Powers for up to Two Years," Toronto Sun (Postmedia Network Inc., July 7, 2020), https://torontosun.com/news/provincial/ford-seeks-emergency-powers-for-up-to-two-years.

We cannot, of course, see inside the mind of Premier Ford so we cannot identify what role his family's criminal past plays in how he views the world now.

It is clear, however, that Premier Ford is not a defender of civil rights. His decision to criminalize those citizens of Ontario who donated to the Freedom Convoy could be explained away as a "fog of war" issue.

However, Premier Ford's decision to change the laws in Ontario with an unscheduled voice vote in the after-hours shows a continuation of his behaviour. His response is typical of an illegitimate leader whose work is only to increase his powers at the cost of the freedoms of those around him.

CHAPTER 21: ASSESSING THE MEDIA'S ROLE IN DECEIT

Trust in the mainstream media has been in a free fall for several years. The problems that plague the media pre-date the Trudeau era and cannot be solely blamed on him. The issue of the digitalization of information has been a factor since at least the mid-1990s.

The relationship between trust in the media, trust in government, and citizens' belief in freedom and democracy is a complex situation.

The role of the media is, however, key for all of them. A well-functioning media is a critical requirement for a functioning democracy. Freedom and democracy are both required to earn the trust and support of the citizenry for the media and government.

In 2021, *only 35% of Canadians said they trusted traditional media*, compared to 38% in the previous year. Only 44% of people put faith in journalists to provide reliable information.[156]

The CTV, CBC, TVA, and the Globe & Mail all scored below 50% in trust ratings in 2021.

At the same time, governments in Canada saw a 10% drop in trust for 2021-2022. Currently, *only 22% of Canadians saw governments of all levels as trustworthy* – down from 32% the year before.[157]

---

[156] Cosmin Dzsurdzsa, "Poll Shows Trust in Media, Government at All-Time Low," True North (True North Centre for Public Policy, February 10, 2022), https://tnc.news/2022/02/10/poll-shows-trust-in-media-government-at-all-time-low/. **Rated B2**

Coincident with these two issues was the question of how Canadians feel about freedom in their country. In 2022, Canadians reported a striking decline of 13% when it came to how free they felt their country was. In 2020, 73% of Canadians said the country was performing well about the core value of freedom, but in 2022 that number had shrunk to 60%.

In 2020, 65% of Canadians were satisfied with its democratic values while in 2022, only 54% of respondents reported the same belief.

Buying the Press

The Government of Canada currently funds the CBC to the tune of $1.394 billion a year, according to their 2020-2021 annual report.[158]

The Government of Canada also has provided some $600 million to the mainstream press – at least those organizations selected by the government-appointed 'independent panel' itself.[159] These tax breaks and

---

[157] MacLellan, Bruce, and Vanessa Eaton. "2022 Proof Strategies CanTrust Index: Summary of Findings." Toronto, Montreal, Ottawa and Washington DC: Proof Strategies, January 2022. **Not Rated.**

[158] Editors, "Financial Sustainability - Revenue and Other Sources of Funds," CBC 2020-2021 Annual Report (CBC Radio-Canada, 2021), https://cbc.radio-canada.ca/en/impact-and-accountability/finances/annual-reports/ar-2020-2021/financial-sustainability/revenue-and-other-funds. Not **Rated**.

[159] Peter Zimonjic, "Federal Government Names Organizations That Will Help Spend $600m Journalism Fund, CBC News | Politics (CBC Radio-Canada, May 24, 2019), https://www.cbc.ca/news/politics/journalism-support-fund-panel-1.5144282. **Rated C3.**

incentives are supposed to assist media organizations to make the transition from the analog age to the digital age.

The reality, however, is that many Canadians, including some journalists, see the $600 million program as little more than an attempt to buy off the media. The mainstream media is now becoming 'state media' in the eyes of many citizens.

Freedom Convoy 2022

As noted in earlier chapters, much of the reporting generated by the CBC and the rest of the mainstream media was false or at least heavily biased. Stories concerning 'terrorist funding' in GoFundMe or GiveSendGo were false. The idea that Russia was somehow behind the Convoy was simply manufactured with no evidence. The proposition that big American money was funding the Convoy was similarly dismissed.

The mainstream media complained about a lack of availability to the Freedom Convoy, but when invited to a presentation (Doctor's Conference) not a single person showed up.

Assessment

Trust in the media in Canada was already low before the Convoy.

However, as one commentator in Canada stated, the media's handling of the Freedom Convoy was "one-sided, inflammatory, (and) shameful."[160]

---

[160] Brian Lilley, "Media's Handling of Trucker Convoy One-Sided, Inflammatory, Shameful," Toronto Sun (Postmedia Network Inc., January 28, 2022),

When the long-term effects of the Freedom Convoy are studied in the future, the mainstream media will probably be noted for having damaged their already low reputation for integrity.

---

https://torontosun.com/opinion/columnists/lilley-medias-handling-of-trucker-convoy-one-sided-inflammatory-shameful. **Rated B3.**

CHAPTER 22: ETHICAL COLLAPSE AND THE GOVERNMENT'S PROGRAM OF DECEIT

Professor Marianne Jennings is a professor of legal and ethical studies in the Department of Management in the W.P. Carey School of Business at Arizona State University. In her 2006 book *The Seven Signs of Ethical Collapse – Understanding what causes Moral Meltdowns in Organizations... before it's too late*[161,162] she identifies seven signs of collapse from a lifetime spent studying business ethics – and ethical failures. It is believed that these seven signs can also help us identify these very same problems occurring in the political realm. Let's apply Jennings' seven signs of ethical collapse to what we have noted occurring within the Trudeau minority Liberal government since early 2022:

1. **Pressure to maintain numbers:** In politics, the opinion poll is king. Politicians live and die by their poll numbers, all too often making difficult, and in many cases, poor decisions based on their maintaining good public opinion poll numbers;

2. **Fear and silence:** In Canadian federal party politics, what the party leader says, goes. The current Liberal Party whip, the Honourable Steven

---

[161] Marianne M. Jennings, *The Seven Signs of Ethical Collapse: How to Spot Moral Meltdowns in Companies... before It's Too Late* (New York, NY: St. Martin's Press, 2006). **Not Rated**
[162] Editors, "Jennings' Seven Signs of Ethical Collapse," YouTube.com (Google LLC, December 13, 2021), https://youtu.be/7HcPJMb02Wg. **Not Rated.**

MacKinnon[163] (28 October 2021 to the Present date), and before him, the Honourable Mark Holland[164] (31 August 2018 to 15 August 2021) were responsible for ensuring elected party members voted along party lines. Should elected party members not vote following the party line, or speak out in opposition to the party policies, they can arbitrarily be removed from whatever roles they fill within their party and government, and potentially be expelled from their party caucus, becoming an independent Member of Parliament. This was the case for the Honourable Jody Wilson-Raybould[165], former Liberal Member of Parliament for Vancouver Granville, and the Honourable Jane Philpott, the former Liberal Member of Parliament for Markham-Stouffville, who were expelled from the Liberal caucus on 2 April 2019 and as candidates for the 2019 fall election by Prime Minister Justin Trudeau, "saying their criticism of his role in the SNC-Lavalin

---

[163] Editors, "The Honourable Steven Mackinnon," Members of Parliament - House of Commons of Canada (Government of Canada, September 20, 2021), https://www.ourcommons.ca/members/en/steven-mackinnon(88468)/roles. **Rated B2.**

[164] Editors, "The Honourable Mark Holland," Members of Parliament - House of Commons of Canada (Government of Canada, September 20, 2021), https://www.ourcommons.ca/members/en/mark-holland(25508)/roles. **Rated B2.**

[165] Editors, "The Honourable Jody Wilson-Raybould," Members of Parliament - House of Commons of Canada (Government of Canada, September 20, 2021), https://www.ourcommons.ca/Members/en/jody-wilson-raybould(89494)/roles. **Rated B2.**

affair had broken bonds of trust and helped the government's political opponents." [166]

3. **Young 'uns and a larger-than-life CEO:** Prime Minister Justin Trudeau followed in the footsteps of his late father, Pierre Elliott Trudeau, former Prime Minister of Canada when he was first elected to Parliament on 14 October 2008. He subsequently became leader of the Liberal party on 15 April 2013, and Prime Minister of Canada on 4 November 2015. He has been a favourite of mainstream media since entering federal politics, although this has declined in recent years due to political scandals such as the SNC Lavalin affair and Freedom Convoy 2022. How does a new/young Liberal Member of Parliament compete with someone like Justin Trudeau; the answer is you just don't.

4. **A weak board of directors:** This is a given, as the current Liberal minority government had to make a governance deal with the New Democratic Party to avoid losing any potential non-confidence votes in the House of Commons. That, plus there are only a few experienced senior members of the party available to fill key ministerial roles in a weak Trudeau government.

---

[166] Robert Fife, Steven Chase, and Janice Dickson, "Trudeau Expels Wilson-Raybould and Philpott from Liberal Caucus over SNC-Lavalin Affair," The Globe and Mail (The Globe and Mail, October 2, 2019), https://www.theglobeandmail.com/politics/article-wilson-raybould-says-she-was-ejected-from-liberal-caucus-stripped-of/. **Rated B1.**

5. **Conflicts:** When Parliament is in session, one can see the constant state of conflict between the political party in power forming the current government and the official opposition party. Conflicts are many, ranging from proposed legislation by the government that the official opposition does not agree with, to major political scandals such as the SNC Lavalin affair.

6. **Innovation like no other:** The current Liberal minority government has chosen to "rule by mandate" in response to the SARS-CoV-2 or COVID-19 global pandemic. This also saw the Liberal government invoke the Emergencies Act[167] for the first time in its history to deal with Freedom Convoy 2022.[168]

7. **Belief that the goodness in some areas atones for wrongdoing in others:** The Trudeau government continues to believe that whatever legislation and mandates that they pursue are for the good of all Canadians. An example of this is Bill C-11, also known as the Digital Charter Implementation Act[169], 2020, or the Online

---

[167] Legislative Services Branch, "Emergencies Act, R.S.C., 1985, c. 22 (4th Supp.)," Justice Laws Website (Government of Canada, May 13, 2022), https://laws-lois.justice.gc.ca/eng/acts/e-4.5/page-1.html. **Rated B2.**

[168] Catharine Tunney, "Federal Government Invokes Emergencies Act for First Time Ever in Response to Protests, Blockades," CBC News Politics (CBC/Radio Canada, February 14, 2022), https://www.cbc.ca/news/politics/trudeau-premiers-cabinet-1.6350734. **Rated C1.**

[169] Editors, "Charter Statement Bill C-11: An Act to Enact the Consumer Privacy Protection Act and the Personal Information and Data Protection Tribunal Act and to Make

Streaming Act. The Trudeau government believes that this legislation will ultimately protect all Canadians in their online activities. However, this bill is seen by many as the legal implementation of the potential censorship of Canadians publishing anything online in social media and independent news fora. Seven times in recent years Liberal Member of Parliament and Minister Steven Guilbeault has attacked free speech[170] Similarly, the Trudeau government continues to enact increasingly more restrictive firearm ownership legislation when Canadians believe that the real problem is illegal firearms being smuggled into Canada daily.[171] An example of this smuggling was a large drone found in a tree located on the bank of the St. Clair River, with an attached bag containing 11 handguns.[172]

Related and Consequential Amendments to Other Acts," Government of Canada (Department of Justice, Electronic Communications, September 1, 2021), https://www.justice.gc.ca/eng/csj-sjc/pl/charter-charte/c11.html. **Rated B2.**

[170] Cosmin Dzsurdzsa, "Seven Times Steven Guilbeault Has Attacked Free Speech," True North (True North Centre for Public Policy, April 20, 2022), https://tnc.news/2022/04/20/seven-times-steven-guilbeault-has-attacked-free-speech/. **Not Rated**

[171] Beatrice Britneff, "Majority of Canadians Support New Gun Ban but Want Feds to Focus on Smuggling: Ipsos," Global News Politics (Global News, a division of Corus Entertainment Inc. Corus News, May 28, 2020), https://globalnews.ca/news/6982152/canadians-gun-ban-ipsos-poll/. **Rated C2.**

[172] Gerry Dewan, "Drone Carrying 11 Guns Found Stuck in Tree near Canada-U.S. Border along St. Clair River," CTV News

Legislation of this nature continues to be pushed by the Trudeau government, whether the public wants it or not.

Summary

Professor Jennings' *Seven Signs of Ethical Collapse* are easily observable from outside the Canadian government by the public and do not require first-person, primary sources to confirm these signs, as the information is easily available through mainstream and independent media and on government websites.

London (Bell Media, May 2, 2022), https://london.ctvnews.ca/drone-carrying-11-guns-stuck-in-a-tree-near-canada-u-s-border-1.5884653. **Rated B2.**

CHAPTER 23: ASSESSING THE GOVERNMENT'S CAMPAIGN OF DECEIT

The Canadian Government ran a malicious campaign of deceit against the Freedom Convoy 2022. This process started before the Convoy arrived in Ottawa and it continued after the Convoy was broken up by force.

The Biggest Lie

The greatest single abuse of human rights in Canada since World War II was likely the imposition of the Emergencies Act on 14 February 2022. The act was imposed by the Trudeau Government, more out of spite and vindictiveness than any degree of necessity. The border blockades were gone, and no one had been injured or killed because of the protests.

According to various officials of the Government of Canada, the act was imposed at the request of "law enforcement."

This, as it turns out, appears to have been a calculated lie.

Consider the following. Prime Minister Trudeau stated:

> *"When illegal blockades hurt workers and endangered public safety, police were clear that they needed tools not held by any federal, provincial or territorial law," Trudeau said on Apr. 27. "It was only after we got advice from law enforcement that we invoked the Emergencies Act."* [173]

---

[173] Cosmin Dzsurdzsa, "No 'Direct Request' for Emergencies Act, Ottawa Police Chief Says," True North (True North Centre for Public Policy, May 17, 2022),

Public Safety Minister Marco Mendicino stated at least six times[174] that the Emergencies Act was brought in only after police requested it. One of those statements was:

> *"We had to invoke the Emergencies Act and we did so on the basis of non-partisan professional advice from law enforcement."*

Two similar statements by Minster Mendicino were:

> *"We had to invoke the Emergencies Act and we did so on the basis of non-partisan professional advice from law enforcement,"* and

> *"It was only after we got advice from law enforcement that we invoked the Emergencies Act."*

Similar claims about the police being required were also made by Finance Minister Chrystia Freeland and Emergency Preparedness Minister Bill Blair.

As it turns out, a series of serving and former heads of police services have stated that they did not request the use of the Emergency Act.

The following can be stated:

The Prime Minister, the Deputy Prime Minster/Finance Minister, the Justice Minister, the Minister of Public Safety, and the Emergency Preparedness Minister all

---

https://tnc.news/2022/05/17/no-direct-request-for-emergencies-act-ottawa-police-chief-says/. **Rated B2**

[174] Lorne Gunter, "Gunter: Yet More Liberal Falsehoods Surrounding the Convoy Have Been Debunked," Toronto Sun (Postmedia Network Inc., May 14, 2022), https://torontosun.com/opinion/columnists/gunter-yet-more-liberal-falsehoods-surrounding-the-convoy-have-been-debunked. **Rated B3.**

lied to Parliament, the media, and/or the citizens of Canada to illegally impose the Emergencies Act to satisfy their political positions.

Any further legal actions deriving from the Freedom Convoy 2022 will be tainted. The most senior officials in law enforcement and justice have willfully lied to the public on a repeated basis, casting into doubt the integrity of the legal cases being pursued against those being charged.

The Aftermath

Senior ministers of Government, such as the Prime Minister, the Justice Minister, and the Minister of Public Safety continue to be caught lying about events and issues months later. The wilful lying to Parliament and the media cannot be considered as anything other than deliberate given the timelines involved. The most disturbing aspect of the lies and deceit is that it comes from the Minister of Public Safety (Chief Law Enforcement Officer) and the Minister of Justice.

Given that the deceit comes from those who are supposedly responsible for law, order, and justice, it calls all of the activities of their agencies in question. Can you trust any of these agencies now? (RCMP, CSIS, Canada Border Services Agency, Parole Board, Corrections Canada, and the Department of Justice).

Propaganda by the State

In 2019, (former) Minister of Environment & Climate Change, Katherine McKenna was caught on video explaining the Government of Canada's approach to lying to the public. In the video, she states:

"I actually gave them some real advice. I said that if you actually say it louder, we've learned in the House of Commons, if you repeat it, if you say it louder, if that is your talking point, people will totally believe it."

Whether Minister McKenna is aware of it or not, she is essentially quoting the approach of Joseph Goebbels who was the Reich Minister of Propaganda in Germany from 1933 to 1945.

Information Warfare

Put into context, it can be reasonably stated that the Government of Canada's program of deceit around Freedom Convoy 2022 is a continuing part of its information war against Canadian citizens.

Under Prime Minister Trudeau, the Government of Canada has taken an entirely new direction in government communications. Rather than a method of communicating ideas and policies to the citizens, the Government now uses information and communications technology as a means of dominating a battle space. In this circumstance, information warfare can be defined as the manipulation of information trusted by a target (the citizens) without the target's awareness. In this way, the target will make decisions and take actions that are in the interests of the Government.

The concept of an information war is that it is a struggle of "perception and information" rather than a kinetic action. The key features are misinformation, social engineering, and the blurring of the lines between war and politics.

The overall information warfare approach by the Government of Canada also incorporates the idea of never allowing the public to cool off. The Government never admits a fault and never allows room for other opinions. The Government always blames someone else for any failures and blames 'enemies' for everything at the same time.[175] This is not a new approach and has been used by leaders with totalitarian approaches in the past.

On one level, it might be reasonable to say that the Government of Canada may have simply reacted poorly to a grassroots protest that did not exist in December of 2021 and yet was a global phenomenon by late January of 2022. Given the overall approach taken by the Government of Canada, however, this cannot be said to be the case. It is a case of information warfare by the Government of Canada against its own citizens.

For those who say the idea that Canada would use information warfare against its own citizens, it should be remembered that this very idea was already underway in 2015, the first year that Prime Minister Trudeau was in power. According to the Ottawa Citizen, the defence minister was advocating such an approach:

> "Sajjan had originally approved the weaponization of public affairs initiative, started in 2015, along with a separate but significant expansion of military propaganda capabilities for various units. The Liberals outlined in their 2017 defence strategy

---

[175] Langer, Walter C. "A Psychological Analysis of Adolf Hitler: His Life and Legend." Washington DC: Office of Strategic Services, 1943.

policy the need for the Canadian military to become more involved in propaganda and information warfare."[176]

---

[176] David Pugliese, "Canadian Military Wants to Establish New Organization to Use Propaganda ...," Ottawa Citizen (Postmedia Network Inc., November 2, 2020), https://ottawacitizen.com/news/national/defence-watch/canadian-military-to-establish-new-organization-to-use-propaganda-other-techniques-to-influence-canadians. **Rated B2.**

CHAPTER 24: FUTURE OUTLOOK

The Government of Canada's campaign of deceit against Freedom Convoy 2022 was instructive. Five of the more significant revelations were:

- From the outset and well after Freedom Convoy 2022 was dispersed, the Prime Minister and Ministers of the Crown blatantly lied to Parliament on the public on multiple issues.

- The Government of Canada willfully lied to the population about the imposition of the Emergencies Act, claiming that it was requested by police when it was not.[177]

- The Prime Minister maintained a vitriolic campaign of hate towards the Convoy and its supporters.

- Large numbers of Canadians from coast to coast to coast supported the Convoy against the will of the Government of Canada.

- The Government of Canada did not, and perhaps could not, meet with the Convoy due to its inability to produce any scientific evidence to support its actions.

Two Minutes Hate

---

[177] The Commissioner of the RCMP, two Ottawa police chiefs and the police chief from neighbouring Gatineau have all stated they did not request the Emergencies Act.

In George Orwell's famous book *1984*, the concept of Two Minutes Hate arises. Party members must daily listen to a statement from Big Brother who expresses his hatred for enemies of "The Party." It is an opportunity for the leader and his followers to vent their anguish and personal hatred for whoever is determined to be an enemy of the state at that moment. It is also a way of having the citizens distracted away from their problems to focusing their hate on 'the other.'

Prime Minister Trudeau appears to have taken a lesson from Orwell's classic book. When addressing anyone who opposes his views, he falls into the habit of applying hateful labels to opponents and then discounts them based on these labels. In this way, he draws attention away from the issues at hand and focuses hate and distraction on others. Consider his statement in the House of Commons concerning the Convoy:

> *"Today in the House, Members of Parliament unanimously condemned the antisemitism, Islamophobia, anti-Black racism, homophobia, and transphobia that we've seen on display in Ottawa over the past number of days."*

In another statement, he refers to those who are "often misogynistic and racist" and that "But they take up space. And with that, we have to make a choice, in terms of a leader as a country. ***Do we tolerate these people***?" (Emphasis added.)

Consciously or not, Prime Minister Trudeau was channeling the worst aspects of dictators when he questions the idea of whether we should tolerate "these people" who "take up space." Bill Mahar, speaking on his Real Time Show on HBO repeated Prime

Minster Trudeau's comments and stated: "You do sound like Hitler."[178]

In short, Prime Minister Trudeau is attempting to use his position as Prime Minister to create an atmosphere of hate, fear, and loathing for working-class Canadians. Common to many globalists/elitists, Prime Minister Trudeau sees the middle and lower classes not as people who have lives and dreams, but as assets to be managed.

Toronto Star

In keeping with the Two Minutes Hate approach to communications, the Toronto Star launched a vicious attack on those in favour of bodily autonomy and freedom of choice. Above the fold on the front page of the Toronto Star of August 26th 2021, the following statements were printed:

- If an unvaccinated person catches it from someone who is vaccinated, boohoo, too bad.

- I have no empathy left for the willfully unvaccinated. Let them die.

- I honestly don't care if they die from COVID. Not even a little bit.

- Unvaccinated patients do not deserve ICU beds. At this point, who cares.

---

[178] Richard Moorhead, "Bill Maher Uncovers Chilling Trudeau Quote, Says 'You Do Sound like Hitler'," The Western Journal, February 14, 2022, https://www.westernjournal.com/bill-maher-uncovers-chilling-trudeau-quote-says-sound-like-hitler/. **Not Rated**

- Stick the unvaccinated in a tent outside and tend to them when the staff has time.

Below the fold, the Toronto Star then went on to say that these were a selection of recent posts on Twitter. Why the Star that it was necessary to make a headline out of such hateful comments is not clear. It does, however, show how the media did, and will likely continue, to support the Government of Canada in its campaign of dividing Canadians and encouraging hate while doing it.

How should we think about the refusal of the Government of Canada to even address Freedom Convoy and its decision to create a false narrative which was used to falsely justify the imposition of the Emergencies Act?

The response of the Government of Canada to the Freedom Convoy 2022 should be considered in the overall agenda of Prime Minister Trudeau and the Liberal Party. This agenda had been at play for more than six years when the Convoy arrived in Ottawa.

Freedom Convoy 2022 was the first physical and visual manifestation of the increasing resistance of Canadians towards Prime Minister Trudeau. The presence of Freedom Convoy 2022 identified the increasing slide towards authoritarianism and the centralization of power undertaken by Prime Minister Trudeau and its all-powerful PMO – the Prime Minister's Office.

Prime Minister Justin Trudeau did not address the Convoy because he could not. Any form of discussion or debate would have led to the point where it was obvious that there was no 'science' behind the mandates against the truckers. It would have also exposed that there was no science or reason behind most of the coercive and restrictive measures undertaken by the Prime Minister.

The Future

The imposition of highly restrictive measures against truckers by the Trudeau government was just one small measure in a larger campaign.

Regardless of what terminology is applied, Prime Minister Trudeau is moving Canada towards a centrally controlled state where all power is concentrated in one office, the PMO. Any organization or institution with influence must either bend to the will of the government or face its wrath.

Those policies and ideas which support a globalist agenda with further elite capture will flourish while ideas that address ideas of freedom or democracy will be attacked.

Currently, Prime Minister Trudeau is advancing his 'progressive' agenda on multiple fronts. Among the most damaging developments are:

- The destruction of the fossil fuel industry;
- Control of the Internet, including user-generated content;
- Attacks on freedom of speech and assembly;
- Increased debt and taxes;
- Weakening the middle class into dependency;
- Increasing use of the politics of identity;
- Open borders;

- Weakening of Canadian sovereignty;

- Politicization of civil society institutions;

- Attacks on religion – especially Christianity;

- Loss of autonomy for doctors;

- Criminalization of law-abiding citizens; (guns owners as an example)

- Critical Race Theory, and

- Modern Monetary Theory.

Conclusion

Canada is facing an uncertain future.

Several narratives advanced by Prime Minister Trudeau are facing collapse and the fallout may be catastrophic for some. Among them are:

Economic Collapse: Canada has engaged in a massive act of capital destruction over the last seven years. Personal and government debts are at an all-time high. The next recession, already beginning, will be destructive to the middle and lower classes. Widespread civil unrest will be a reality.

Corruption: The systemic corruption in Canada has become so pervasive that it is now fair to ask the question of whether the Government of Canada is in the looting phase of societal collapse.

Societal Collapse: The Trudeau social agenda has been driven by open borders and the destruction of traditional Canadian values with no viable replacement. Wars between borders will be replaced by wars between neighbourhoods.

Democratic Deficits and Social Trust: The undermining of trust in the institutions of civil society is growing. Among those most damaged are government, the media, the financial sector, the medical sector, education, and law enforcement. This is another determinant of social unrest.

The Vaccine Mandates: The population is only now beginning to figure out the ineffectiveness of the COVID-19 mRNA vaccines. At the same time, the damage done by the mRNA vaccines is becoming apparent as the early indicators of death and injury are proving to be true. *Once the population understands the enormity of the damage, both the health care sector and government may be forcibly restructured.*

Canada has been blessed with natural resources, space, and a generally productive population. If the development of those resources and personnel can be effectively developed, then Canada could still be a prosperous and democratic country. At the same time, Canada could help address weaknesses and imbalances overseas with an effective energy policy.

If, however, the current path toward globalism, elitism, and progressivism continues, Canada will continue down a path towards deprivation. While many call Prime Minister Trudeau a "Hitler" or a "Stalin," these labels are neither accurate nor helpful in understanding the future of Canada.

It should be remembered that both Prime Minister Justin Trudeau and his 'coalition partner' Jagmeet Singh are huge admirers of Fidel Castro and South American forms of Marxism and socialism. Can anything be learned from that?

Those who wish to have insights into where Canada is going may look toward Venezuela. An energy-rich country that had a growing middle class with a generally peaceful society was destroyed. Hugo Chavez was elected (legally) in 1999. It took him less than a decade to turn Venezuela into a disarmed society, riven by violence, crime, corruption, and inflation which resulted in a mass exodus of the population. The country is now in ruins and economic recovery remains a dream. With an inflation rate of 686% in 2021, it is unclear if Venezuela will recover in the next decade.

Will Canada become the next Venezuela?

APPENDIX A: REVISED AND UPDATED ADMIRALTY RATING SYSTEM FOR SOURCE RELIABILITY AND INFORMATION CREDIBILITY

R.L.A. (Rick) Gill, CD

Key Points

- Since its initial development in the 1940s during World War Two, the original UK Admiralty rating system for source reliability and information credibility has remained unchanged in its original form until 2006.

- Little or no details have ever been provided on the use of the UK Admiralty rating system. Coupled with users' tendencies to correlate source reliability ratings with information credibility ratings, these factors have led to little or no use of this rating system in recent years.

- Revisions to this rating system first began appearing in 2006 in U.S., NATO and other national military doctrinal and open-source publications have begun to make useful improvements to this (now) seven-decade-old rating system.

- This revised and updated version of the original UK Admiralty rating system serves to allow users to better choose and identify the reliability of their sources and credibility of those sources' information for readers of their reports and publications.

Recent Events

The first noted changes to the original 1940s era UK Admiralty rating system were published in 2006, in a new and publicly available U.S. Army Field Manual (FM) 2-22.3 "Human Intelligence Collector Operations." The changes included questions and issues to be considered by users when selecting source reliability and information credibility ratings.

In 2010, Canadian analytic methodologists (including the author) began to make further revisions to the original UK Admiralty rating system, based on the questions and issues mentioned in FM2-22.3 to be considered by users when selecting source reliability and information accuracy (credibility) ratings. Our intent was to provide an improved process allowing users to make better choices for ratings to be applied to analytic products.

In his 2010 book, *Scientific Methods of Inquiry for Intelligence Analysis*, Dr. Hank Prunckun[179] addressed the issue of rating information believed to be either "misinformation" or "disinformation." A revised and updated Admiralty rating system was published in 2012[180],

---

[179] "Dr. Henry Prunckun," Henry Prunckun - Australian Graduate School of Policing and Security (Charles Sturt University, June 1, 2021), https://bjbs.csu.edu.au/schools/agsps/staff/profiles/adjunct-staff/hank_prunckun. **Rated A1.**
[180] "U.S. Army Techniques Publication (ATP) 2-22.9 Open-

in a new U.S. Army publication dealing with Open-Source Intelligence (OSINT), in which the modified rating system appears to have been influenced by the work of Dr. Prunckun. These additional questions and issues to be considered by users when selecting ratings, as seen in the U.S. Army's FM 2-22.3 and later ATP 2.22-9, began to appear in NATO and other allied nations' doctrinal publications.

In the second edition of *Scientific Methods of Inquiry for Intelligence Analysis*[181] published in 2015, Dr. Prunckun expanded upon his earlier work, addressing issues related to the potential for deception by the source, in addition to misinformation and disinformation. He did this by including additional ratings in both source and information categories to indicate:

- A source that is either "unintentionally misleading" or "deliberately deceptive," and

- Information which is either "misinformation" or "disinformation."

Source Intelligence," An Army Introduction to Open Source Intelligence (Federation Of American Scientists Secrecy News, September 13, 2012),
https://fas.org/blogs/secrecy/2012/09/army_osint/ **Rated A1.**
[181] Hank Prunckun, "Scientific Methods of Inquiry for Intelligence Analysis, Second Edition," Rowman & Littlefield (Rowman & Littlefield, September 2014),
https://rowman.com/ISBN/9781442224315/Scientific-Methods-of-Inquiry-for-Intelligence-Analysis-Second-Edition ,
53-54 **Rated A1.**

In this second edition, Dr. Prunckun included new source ratings of F-G and information ratings of 6-7, pushing back the original "F" and "6" ratings of "Cannot be Judged" to "H" and "8", respectively. I believe that this change causes issues of backward compatibility with the original Admiralty rating system, for its many long-time military and other users, who easily remember the meaning of a rating of "F6" as "source reliability and information credibility cannot be judged."

My initial thoughts on adopting Dr. Prunckun's additions to the Admiralty rating system were to leave "F" and "6" where they were in the UK Admiralty rating system and added his additional ratings for "Unintentionally Misleading" (F) and "Deliberately Deceptive" (G) for source reliability, and "Misinformation" (6) and "Deception" (7) below "F" and "6". These modifications would retitle his additional ratings to "Unintentionally Misleading" (G) and "Deliberately Deceptive" (H) for source reliability, and "Misinformation" (7) and "Deception" (8). This modification to Dr. Prunckun's revised UK Admiralty rating system would now keep his revisions backwardly compatible with the original UK Admiralty rating system.

Subsequent discussions with colleagues in Canada's Defence Research and Development, and Security and Intelligence communities led me to conclude that Dr. Prunckun's ratings and descriptions of "Unintentionally Misleading" (F) and "Deliberately Deceptive" (G) for source reliability, and "Misinformation" (6) and "Deception" (7) were regarded as subsets of the categories "Unreliable (E) and "Improbable" (5). Dr. Prunckun's descriptions for his additional ratings of "Unintentionally Misleading" and "Deliberately Deceptive" for source reliability, and "Misinformation" and "Deception" have now been included under "Unreliable" (E) and "Improbable" (5) in the revised UK Admiralty rating system used in this publication.

Background

The first known source reliability and information accuracy (credibility) rating system was developed by the UK Royal Navy's Admiralty staff during the Battle of the Atlantic in World War Two. The Admiralty staff needed a method by which they could systematically evaluate, and rate mass volumes of reporting being received from a wide variety of sources. What quickly became known as the Admiralty Source Reliability and Information Accuracy rating system (shown below) was developed at that time and subsequently adopted for use in subsequent years by British and other NATO military forces.

Evaluation of Source Reliability		Evaluation of Information Accuracy	
Code	Description	Code	Description
A	Reliable	1	Confirmed
B	Usually Reliable	2	Probably True
C	Fairly Reliable	3	Possibly True
D	Not Usually Reliable	4	Doubtfully True
E	Unreliable	5	Improbable

Evaluation of Source Reliability		Evaluation of Information Accuracy	
F	Cannot be Judged	6	Cannot be Judged

A report or information received would be rated for source reliability and information accuracy by a combination of the letter-number codes shown above. For example:

A report or information received from a source that is **"usually reliable"** and whose information provided at that point in time is believed to be **"probably true"** would be rated as **"B2"**.

Since its initial development, the original Admiralty rating system shown above has been published in British, U.S., Canadian, and other NATO nations' doctrinal publications "as-is" for nearly six decades. Other than one or two examples like that provided above, the Admiralty rating system in these various doctrinal publications was accompanied by little or no explanation on how to effectively select ratings using this system.

Research, Revisions, and Updates

U.S. Army research[182] conducted in 1975 on the use of the Admiralty rating system conducted found:

---

[182] Michael G. Samet, "Subjective Interpretation of Reliability and Accuracy Scales for Evaluating Military Intelligence," DTIC (U.S. Army Research Institute for the Behavioral and Social Sciences, January 1, 1975),

"About one-fourth of the [37] subjects treated reliability and accuracy as independent dimensions; the majority treated reliability as highly correlated with accuracy, and their judgement of a report's truth was influenced more strongly by its accuracy rating. Numerical (probabilistic) interpretations of scale levels were consistent within individuals but varied widely between them. <u>Development of a new scale is suggested.</u>"

This revised and updated Source Reliability and Information Credibility rating system provided below is an amalgam of the U.S. doctrinal publications discussed above and rearranged additional elements of that published by Dr. Prunckun in 2015. This source reliability and information credibility rating system is backwardly compatible with both the original UK Admiralty rating system, and recent military doctrinal updates to the UK Admiralty rating system. Source reliability and information credibility ratings used in this, and subsequent publications will be indicated in bold, to delineate ratings from a document's content, citations, footnotes, or endnotes. Examples of this are "**rated B2**" (source is usually reliable; information is probably true), "**rated C4**" (source is fairly reliable; however, this information is doubtful), and "**rated F6**" (source reliability and information credibility cannot be judged). This revised source reliability and information credibility rating system tables will be included as an annex or appendix in all publications and other products.

---

https://apps.dtic.mil/sti/citations/ADA003260. **Rated B1.**

Implications

These enhancements to the original UK Admiralty rating system and its use in publications are intended to provide:

a. Analysts with a more consistent method of applying this rating system, and

b. Consumers of analytic products with the best possible understanding of analysts' deliberations on their sources being cited and the information provided by those sources.

Updated Admiralty Rating System: Source Reliability

Code	Description	Issues to be considered by Users when selecting a Rating
A	Completely Reliable	**No doubt** of source's authenticity, trustworthiness, or competency; source has a history of complete reliability.
B	Usually Reliable	**Minor doubt** about source's authenticity, trustworthiness, or competency; source has a history of valid information most of the time.

Code	Description	Issues to be considered by Users when selecting a Rating
C	**Fairly Reliable**	**Doubt** of source's authenticity, trustworthiness, or competency, but source has provided valid information in the past.
D	**Not Usually Reliable**	**Significant doubt** about source's authenticity, trustworthiness, or competency, but source has provided valid information in the past.
E	**Unreliable**	**Lacking authenticity, trustworthiness, and competency**; the source has a history of invalid information. Alternately, the source is **unintentionally misleading** or **deliberately deceptive**, having been contradicted by other independent and reliable sources on the same subject.
F	**Reliability Cannot Be Judged**	**No basis** exists for evaluating the reliability of the source.

In every instance, the ratings above are based on previous reporting from that source. If there has been no prior reporting this source, the source must initially be rated "F". **NOTE:** An "F" rating does not mean that the source cannot be trusted, but that there is no reporting history and therefore no basis for making any other determination.

Updated Admiralty Rating System: Info Credibility

Code	Description	Issues to be considered by Users when selecting a Rating
1	Confirmed by Other Sources	<u>Confirmed by other independent sources</u>; logical by itself; consistent with other information on the subject.
2	Probably True	<u>Not confirmed</u>; logical by itself; consistent with other information on the subject.
3	Possibly True	<u>Not confirmed</u>; reasonably logical by itself; agrees with some other information on the subject.
4	Doubtful	<u>Not confirmed</u>; possible but not logical; no other information on the subject.

Code	Description	Issues to be considered by Users when selecting a Rating
5	Improbable	<u>Not confirmed</u>; not logical by itself; contradicted by other information on the subject. Alternately, the information is <u>unintentionally false</u> or <u>deliberately false</u>, having been **contradicted by other independent and confirmed information** on the same subject.
6	**Truth Cannot Be Judged**	No basis exists for evaluating the validity of the information.

The highest degree of confidence in reported information (1) is given when confirmed by other independently verified sources. The table above provides the evaluated ratings for information credibility. The degree of confidence decreases if the information is not confirmed, and/or is not logical. *The evaluated rating of 5 means the information is evaluated as false: unintentionally or deliberately.* A rating of "6" does not necessarily mean false information but is generally used to indicate that no determination of credibility can be made since the information is new and not previously received from other sources.

APPENDIX B: MIS-INFORMATION, DIS-INFORMATION AND MAL-INFORMATION

Key Points

- Collectively, misinformation, disinformation and (now) malinformation are spoken of as "information disorder";

- In addition to mainstream media, misinformation, disinformation, and malinformation are quickly and easily disseminated via today's numerous channels of social media;

- These many channels of dissemination lead us to constant information overload; which in turn, we have no choice but to filter out a great deal of available information;

- Cognitive biases such as confirmation bias (simply put, something that confirms what we already believe) play a large part in the ease of the dissemination of misinformation, disinformation, and malinformation.

To understand the subjects of this appendix, we need to briefly review some recent writings on these increasingly important issues. Understanding the key aspects of misinformation, disinformation and malinformation is key to dealing with these problems which we are all confronted with daily.

Claire Wardle currently leads the strategic direction and research for First Draft. In 2017 she co-authored the seminal report Information Disorder: An Interdisciplinary Framework for Research and Policy for the Council of Europe.[183] Wardle has written extensively on the subject of fake news, misinformation, disinformation, and malinformation.

Her February 2017 article "Fake news. It's complicated"[184] provides a very good overview of what she describes as the "misinformation ecosystem." Wardle breaks it down this ecosystem into three elements:

- The different types of content;

- The motivations of the content creators, and

- How this content is disseminated.

Wardle identifies seven types of misinformation and dis-information, which are listed from low to high in terms of their potential for damage. Reviewing these seven types will help readers to understand the complexity of this ecosystem:

- **Satire or parody:** No intent to cause harm but has the potential to fool; (as it does all too often!)

---

[183] Claire Wardle and Hossein Derakhshan, "Information Disorder: Toward an Interdisciplinary Framework for Research and Policy Making," Council of Europe (Council of Europe Publishing, September 27, 2017), https://edoc.coe.int/en/media/7495-information-disorder-toward-an-interdisciplinary-framework-for-research-and-policy-making.html. **Not Rated.**

[184] Claire Wardle, "Fake News. It's Complicated.," First Draft, February 16, 2017, https://firstdraftnews.org/articles/fake-news-complicated/. Article also available in Arabic, French, German and Spanish. **Not Rated.**

- o Examples: https://www.theonion.com and https://www.thebeaverton.com

- **False connection:** When headlines, visuals or captions don't support the content;

- **Misleading content:** Misleading use of information to frame an issue or individual;

- **False context:** When genuine content is shared with false contextual information;

- **Imposter content:** When genuine sources are impersonated;

- **Manipulated content:** When genuine information or imagery is manipulated to deceive, and

- **Fabricated content:** New, original content is 100 percent false, designed to deceive and do harm.

Motivations

In his January 2017 article titled *"Everything you always wanted to know about fake news but were afraid to google,"*[185] author Robert Hackwill quoted Bellingcat founder and creative director Eliot Higgins speaking about "the power that drives fake news" and how Higgins summarized that power with four Ps, *Passion, Politics, Propaganda, and Payment.* Wardle

---

[185] Robert Hackwill, "Everything You Always Wanted to Know about Fake News but Were Afraid to Google," euronews, January 24, 2017, https://www.euronews.com/2017/01/24/everything-you-always-wanted-to-know-about-fake-news-but-were-afraid-to-google. **Rated F6**

subsequently added to Higgins' four Ps and provided her readers with four additional Ps, which altogether are: *Poor Journalism, Parody, to Provoke or 'Punk', Passion, Partisanship, Profit, Political Influence or Power, and Propaganda*. At the time of writing, Wardle stated that her eight Ps were a work in progress but stated that "distinct patterns in terms of the types of content created for specific purposes" would quickly become apparent.

In their 2017 report "Media Manipulation and Disinformation Online"[186] authors Alice Marwick and Rebecca Lewis show us how the mainstream media's dependence on social media, analytics and metrics, sensationalism, novelty over newsworthiness, and clickbait makes them vulnerable to such media manipulation.

Marwick and Lewis also relate how media manipulation has contributed to an exponentially decreasing trust in mainstream media, increased misinformation, and further radicalization of specific target groups and the general public.

Dissemination

In the third element of her information ecosystem, Claire Wardle tells us that we need to think about how misinformation, disinformation and malinformation content is disseminated to its intended target audiences. In addition to mainstream media, today

---

[186] Alice Marwick and Rebecca Lewis, "Media Manipulation and Disinformation Online," Data & Society (Data & Society Research Institute, May 15, 2017), https://datasociety.net/library/media-manipulation-and-disinfo-online/. **Not Rated.**

numerous social media channels play a major role as dissemination mechanisms. In *"Fake news. It's complicated."* Wardle also provided readers with a 3D "misinformation matrix" matching her seven types on mis- and disinformation and her eight Ps of motivation.

Malinformation is a term new to many of us. Wardle describes malinformation as *"genuine information that is shared with an intent to cause harm."* The example provided was that Russian agents hacked into emails from the Democratic National Committee and the Hillary Clinton campaign and leaked certain details to the public to damage reputations.

In her updated 2020 article on these issues, Claire Wardle tells us that *"We live in an age of Information disorder."* [187] Wardle and colleagues collectively refer to misinformation, disinformation and malinformation as *"information disorder".*

Of note, the Communications Security Establishment's Canadian Centre for Cyber Security published an unclassified two-page document "How to Identify Misinformation, Disinformation and Malinformation,"[188] (ITSAP.00.300) in February 2022. In it, misinformation,

---

[187] Claire Wardle, "Understanding Information Disorder," First Draft, September 22, 2020, https://firstdraftnews.org/long-form-article/understanding-information-disorder/. **Not Rated.**

[188] Editors, "How to Identify Misinformation, Disinformation, and Malinformation (ITSAP.00.300)," Canadian Centre for Cyber Security (Government of Canada / Gouvernement du Canada, February 23, 2022), https://cyber.gc.ca/en/guidance/how-identify-misinformation-disinformation-and-malinformation-itsap00300. **Rated B1**

disinformation, and malinformation are collectively referred to as 'MDM'. The CCCS assesses that:

> "The effects of misinformation, disinformation, and malinformation (MDM) cost the global economy billions of dollars each year. Often known colloquially as "fake news", MDM are damaging to public trust in institutions and, during elections, may even pose a threat to democracy itself."

In brief, this document explains to its readers:

- How to identify MDM;
- How consumers can deal with MDM, and
- How organizations can deal with MDM.

Conclusions

Wardle has stated that those working with information of all types urgently need to discuss when, why and how to report on examples of mis- and disinformation, and automated campaigns often used to promote them. Of note, Wardle defines a "tipping point" at which mis- and disinformation become 'beneficial' to address. Wardle offers these 10 questions[189] to kickstart the "when, how and why" discussion mentioned above:

1. Who is our audience? (Or audiences?) (VERY important to know!)

2. When should we publish reports about mis- and dis-information? (For decades, this has consistently been an important question in

---

[189] Claire Wardle, "10 Questions to Ask before Covering Misinformation," First Draft, September 29, 2017, https://firstdraftnews.org/articles/10-questions-newsrooms/. **Not Rated.**

national and international intelligence communities, particularly in the practice of "warning intelligence.")

3. How do we think about the impact of mis- and dis-information, particularly on Twitter?

4. How do we isolate human interactions in a computationally affordable manner?

5. For those of us whose primary goal is to stop mis- and disinformation, (and now malinformation) what strategies of distribution beyond publishing need we consider?

6. How do we write our corrections and updates?

7. Why do we report on attempts at manufactured amplification? (e.g., the use of bots)

8. Who should be talking about manufactured amplification?

9. How should we write about attempts at manufactured amplification?

10. Where do the responsibilities of journalists end and the responsibilities of the intelligence community start?

Today's hyper-connected lifestyles give us access to an immense amount of information of all types, but conversely, make us equally vulnerable to a massive volume of misleading information content. In this article, Wardle states:

"Imposter websites, designed to look like professional outlets, are pumping out misleading hyper-partisan content. Sock puppet accounts post outrage memes to Instagram, and click farms manipulate the trending sections of social media platforms and their recommendation systems. Elsewhere, foreign agents pose as [citizens] to coordinate real-life protests between different communities, while the mass collection of personal data is used to micro-target voters with [customized] messages and advertisements. Over and above this, conspiracy communities on 4chan and Reddit are busy trying to fool reporters into covering rumors or hoaxes."

Wardle and her colleagues at First Draft have provided readers with several essential guides for:

- Newsgathering and monitoring the social web;

- Verifying information online, and

- Closed Groups, Messaging Apps and Online Ads.

Finally, having a better understanding of misinformation, disinformation and malinformation, and how these affect us, will provide us with the advantages required to see through these types of information and ultimately determine the necessary true information needed in our day-to-day lives.

N.B.: Eliot Higgins is the well-known founder and creative director of the very successful online investigative collective known as Bellingcat.[190] On 14

---

[190] Editors, "Bellingcat - The Home of Online Investigations,"

June 2022, First Draft executive director Claire Wardle and Brown University simultaneously announced that First Draft's mission is moving to the Information Futures Lab at Brown University.[191,192]

Bellingcat, March 10, 2022, https://www.bellingcat.com/.
Rated A2.
[191] Claire Wardle, "Update from First Draft Executive Director Claire Wardle," First Draft, June 14, 2022,
https://firstdraftnews.org/first-draft-update-june2022/.
Rated B1
[192] Information Futures Lab, Claire Wardle, and Stefanie Friedhoff, "Brown School of Public Health Launches New Lab to Combat Misinformation, Data Deficits, Outdated Communication Practices - and to Catalyze Innovation," Information Futures Lab (Brown School of Public Health - Brown University, June 14, 2022),
https://sites.brown.edu/informationfutures/2022/06/14/ifl_l aunch-2/. **Rated B1.**

APPENDIX C: FREEDOM CONVOY 2022 EVENT AND SAFETY REPORTS

The reports prepared for Freedom Convoy 2022 can be seen on a Google drive at:
https://drive.google.com/drive/u/0/folders/1PBERG6tDfBGKgsqy2SLVr9iYi4wW8z-7

They consist of the following:

- Great Reset PDF slides, Bank of Canada, 20 August 2020
- FC2022 Intel Report, 7 Jan 2022
- Intel Report, 8 Jan 2022
- FC Violence Warning, 8 Jan 2022
- Daily Intelligence Report, 1 Feb 2022
- Intel Report, 2 Feb 2022
- Special Report - Shepherds of Good Hope, 2 Feb 2022
- Daily Intel Report, 3 Feb 2022
- Potential Violence Warning, 3 Feb 2022
- Daily Intel Report, 4 Feb 2022
- Daily intel report, 5 Feb 2022
- Daily intel report, 6 Feb 2022
- Daily Intel Report, 7 Feb 2022
- Special Report on Faith and Freedom
- Daily Intel Report, 8 Feb 2022

- Special Report on Chief Sloly, 9 Feb 2022
- Daily Intel Report, 9 Feb 2022
- Daily Intel Report, 10 Feb 2022
- Daily Intel Report, 11 Feb 2022
- Daily Intel Report, 12 Feb 2022
- Daily Intel Report, 13 Feb 2022, and
- Daily Intel Brief, 16 Feb 2022.

BIBLIOGRAPHY

Arouet (Voltaire), François-Marie. "Quotes from Work Le Siècle De Louis XIV (Voltaire)." Quotepark.com. Accessed April 3, 2022. https://quotepark.com/works/le-siecle-de-louis-xiv-6902/.

Arouet (Voltaire), François-Marie. "'It Is Dangerous to Be Right in Matters Where Established Men Are Wrong.'." Quotepark.com, June 3, 2021. https://quotepark.com/quotes/1839239-voltaire-it-is-dangerous-to-be-right-in-matters-where-estab/.

Baldwin, Derek. "SIU Probes Reported Injury of Mohawk Woman after Ottawa Incident with Police Horse." The Whig. The Kingston Whig Standard, February 22, 2022. https://www.thewhig.com/news/siu-probes-reported-injury-of-mohawk-woman-in-ottawa-incident-with-police-horse.

Bet-David, Patrick. "Is Justin Trudeau A Coward For Fleeing Canada During Freedom Convoy Protests?" YouTube. Google LLC, February 6, 2022. https://www.youtube.com/watch?v=bZB36C5BGsk.

Blacklock's Reporter. "Public Safety Minister @Marcomendicino Says He Contacted Unnamed Reporters to 'Be Very Careful' in #FreedomConvoy Coverage. Very, Very Careful. Https://T.co/segsvpk0ob #Cdnpoli @safety_canada Pic.twitter.com/jxbyjxr0ey." Twitter. Twitter, February 28, 2022. https://twitter.com/mindingottawa/status/149828 5198651572226?s=20&t=04SzqPmrFT2SSK7H0dWo 5Q.

Blacklock's Reporter. "'Cabinet Wants to Narrow the Year-Long Review Because They Can See Where This Is Going and They'Re Nervous as Hell.' ." Twitter. Twitter, March 31, 2022. https://twitter.com/mindingottawa/status/150949 4990929543173?s=20&t=9COWyIB-mxeInCJdgN0nnA.

Brad. "Canadian Media Cover-up International Condemnation of Justin Trudeau." CAPforCanada.com. Cultural Action Party of Canada, March 9, 2022. https://capforcanada.com/canadian-media-cover-up-international-condemnation-of-justin-trudeau/.

Bradley, Jonathan. "Study Shows Canada's High Pandemic Spending Achieved Low Results." TNC.news. True North Centre for Public Policy, March 1, 2022. https://tnc.news/2022/03/01/study-shows-canadas-high-pandemic-spending-achieved-low-results/.

Busson, Senator Bev. "Topic Intervention 570326 - 1." Senate of Canada. Parliament of Canada, February 23, 2022. https://sencanada.ca/en/senators/busson-bev/interventions/570326/1#hID.

Butts, Gerald. "The Lesson to Take from This Joke Being Torqued by Infowars and Other Alt-Right Nazi Friends of the Rebel Is They're Paying Attention. Game on, #TeamTrudeau." Twitter. Twitter Inc., February 8, 2018. https://twitter.com/gmbutts/status/961573323112 112129.

Cantin-Nantel, Elie. "Cantin-Nantel: I Went to Carleton's 'Journalism under Siege' Event, and the Legacy

Media Know They're Flawed." TNC.news. True
North Centre for Public Policy, March 10, 2022.
https://tnc.news/2022/03/10/cantin-nantel-i-went-
to-carletons-journalism-under-siege-event-and-the-
legacy-media-know-theyre-flawed-2/.

CBC News Team. "Power & Politics - CBC Media Centre."
CBC News. CBC/Radio Canada, 2022.
https://www.cbc.ca/mediacentre/program/power-
politics.

Connolly, Amanda. "Police Arson Unit Probing Alleged
Attempt to Start Fire in Ottawa Apartment Building,
Says Mayor." Global News. Corus Entertainment
Inc. - Corus News., February 8, 2022.
https://globalnews.ca/news/8600592/trucker-
convoy-police-investigating-arson-apartment/.

Corbishley, Nick. "Parts of Spanish Economy Grind to a
Halt after Five-Day Nationwide Truckers' Strike."
Naked Capitalism, March 18, 2022.
https://www.nakedcapitalism.com/2022/03/spanis
h-industry-begins-grinding-to-halt-after-four-day-
nationwide-truckers-strike.html.

Crane, Emily. "Justin Trudeau Moved to Secret Location
during Canada Vax Protests: Report." New York
Post. NYP Holdings, Inc., January 30, 2022.
https://nypost.com/2022/01/30/justin-trudeau-
moved-to-secret-location-during-vax-protests/.

Dotto, Carlotta, and Rory Smith. "Newsgathering and
Monitoring on the Social Web." First Draft,
September 22, 2020.
https://firstdraftnews.org/long-form-
article/newsgathering-and-monitoring-on-the-
social-web/.

Drążkiewicz, Elżbieta. "Study Conspiracy Theories with
Compassion." Nature News. Nature Publishing

Group, March 29, 2022.
https://www.nature.com/articles/d41586-022-00879-w.

Duffy, Andrew, and Elizabeth Payne. "Former Police Board Chair Diane Deans Says She Was Ousted for Not Backing Mayor's Protester Negotiations." Ottawa Citizen. Postmedia Network Inc., February 18, 2022. https://ottawacitizen.com/news/local-news/former-police-board-chair-says-she-was-ousted-for-not-backing-mayors-protester-negotiations.

Durden, Tyler. "People Are Seeing through Holes in Woke Ideology: Critical Theory Expert." ZeroHedge. ABC Media, Ltd., March 16, 2022. https://www.zerohedge.com/political/people-are-seeing-through-holes-woke-ideology-critical-theory-expert.

Dzsurdzsa, Cosmin. "CBC Anchor Invents Conspiracy about Russia Orchestrating Freedom Convoy." True North. True North Centre for Public Policy, January 29, 2022. https://tnc.news/2022/01/29/cbc-anchor-invents-conspiracy-about-russia-orchestrating-freedom-convoy/.

Dzsurdzsa, Cosmin. "DZSURDZSA: How the Liberals and NDP Pushed the Arson Hoax about the Freedom Convoy." True North. True North Centre for Public Policy, April 7, 2022. https://tnc.news/2022/04/07/dzsurdzsa-how-the-liberals-and-ndp-pushed-the-arson-hoax-about-the-freedom-convoy/.

Dzsurdzsa, Cosmin. "Five Times Justin Trudeau Has Ruled Canada by Decree." TNC.news. True North Centre for Public Policy, March 18, 2022.

https://tnc.news/2022/03/18/four-times-justin-trudeau-has-ruled-canada-by-decree/.

Dzsurdzsa, Cosmin. "Liberal MP Compares Freedom Convoy Funding to 'Terrorist Financing.'" True North. True North Centre for Public Policy, February 4, 2022. https://tnc.news/2022/02/04/liberal-mp-compares-freedom-convoy-funding-to-terrorist-financing/.

Dzsurdzsa, Cosmin. "No Evidence of Terrorist Activity during Convoy Protests: RCMP Financial Crime Director." TNC.news. True North Centre for Public Policy, March 17, 2022. https://tnc.news/2022/03/17/no-evidence-of-terrorist-activity-during-convoy-protests-rcmp-financial-crime-director/.

Dzsurdzsa, Cosmin. "No Evidence of Terrorist Activity during Convoy Protests: RCMP Financial Crime Director." TNC.news. True North Centre for Public Policy, March 17, 2022. https://tnc.news/2022/03/17/no-evidence-of-terrorist-activity-during-convoy-protests-rcmp-financial-crime-director/.

Dzsurdzsa, Cosmin. "Ottawa Councillor and Police Chair Calls Convoy 'Treason' and 'Insurrection.'" True North. True North Centre for Public Policy, February 8, 2022. https://tnc.news/2022/02/08/ottawa-councillor-and-police-chair-calls-convoy-treason-and-insurrection/.

Dzsurdzsa, Cosmin. "Ottawa Police Admit Freedom Convoy Unconnected to Arson Attempt." TNC.news. True North Centre for Public Policy, March 21, 2022. https://tnc.news/2022/03/21/ottawa-police-admit-freedom-convoy-unconnected-to-arson-attempt/.

Dzsurdzsa, Cosmin. "Six Times Liberal Claims about the Freedom Convoy Were Officially Disputed." TNC.news. True North Centre for Public Policy, March 24, 2022. https://tnc.news/2022/03/24/six-times-liberal-claims-about-the-freedom-convoy-were-officially-disputed/.

Dzsurdzsa, Cosmin. "Trudeau Invokes Emergencies Act to Quash Canada-Wide Trucker Protests." True North. True North Centre for Public Policy, February 14, 2022. https://tnc.news/2022/02/14/trudeau-invokes-emergencies-act-to-quash-canada-wide-trucker-protests/.

Editors. "Bellingcat - The Home of Online Investigations." Bellingcat, March 10, 2022. https://www.bellingcat.com/.

Editors. "Black Bloc." Counter Extremism Project, 2022. https://www.counterextremism.com/supremacy/black-bloc.

Editors. "Calls Convoy Cash Harmless." Blacklock's Reporter, February 25, 2022. https://www.blacklocks.ca/calls-convoy-cash-harmless/.

Editors. "CBC Corrects Kremlin Story." Blacklock's Reporter. 1395804 Ontario Ltd, February 4, 2022. https://www.blacklocks.ca/cbc-corrects-kremlin-claim/.

Editors. "Convoy Arson Story Is False." Blacklock's Reporter, March 22, 2022. https://www.blacklocks.ca/convoy-arson-story-is-false/.

Editors. "Convoy Claims Contradicted." Blacklock's Reporter. 1395804 Ontario Ltd, March 25, 2022. https://www.blacklocks.ca/convoy-claims-contradicted/.

Editors. "Evidence - Just (42-1) - No. 132 - House of Commons of Canada." Standing Committee on Justice and Human Rights meeting - House of Commons of Canada. Government of Canada, February 21, 2019. https://www.ourcommons.ca/DocumentViewer/en/42-1/just/meeting-132/evidence.

Editors. "False Convoy Claim Repeated." Blacklock's Reporter, April 27, 2022. https://www.blacklocks.ca/false-convoy-claim-repeated/.

Editors. "How to Identify Misinformation, Disinformation, and Malinformation (ITSAP.00.300)." Canadian Centre for Cyber Security. Government of Canada / Gouvernement du Canada, February 23, 2022. https://cyber.gc.ca/en/guidance/how-identify-misinformation-disinformation-and-malinformation-itsap00300.

Editors. "Likens Truckers To Terrorists." Blacklock's Reporter, February 11, 2022. https://www.blacklocks.ca/likens-truckers-to-terrorists/.

Editors. "Organizing against the Occupation of Ottawa." Punch Up Collective, February 6, 2022. https://www.punchupcollective.org/2022/02/06/organizing-against-the-occupation-of-ottawa/.

Editors. "Public Safety Minister Discusses Security Concerns around Protest Convoy." CBC News. YouTube, January 28, 2022. https://www.youtube.com/watch?v=MLKcfi9WLXA.

Editors. "Trudeau Says 'Fringe Minority' in Trucker Convoy with 'Unacceptable Views' Don't Represent Canadians." Global News. Corus Entertainment Inc.

Corus News, January 27, 2022.
https://globalnews.ca/video/8542159/trudeau-
says-fringe-minority-in-trucker-convoy-with-
unacceptable-views-dont-represent-canadians.
Editors. "Trudeau Says He's Isolating after Exposure to
COVID-19." CBC News Politics. CBC/Radio Canada,
January 27, 2022.
https://www.cbc.ca/news/politics/trudeau-
isolation-covid-1.6329476.
Editors. "Why We Tend to Rely Heavily upon the First
Piece of Information We Receive - Anchoring Bias
Explained." The Decision Lab, 2022.
https://thedecisionlab.com/biases/anchoring-bias.
Faulkner, Harrison. "Recap of Day 12 of Truckers for
Freedom Convoy across Canada." True North. True
North Centre for Public Policy, February 3, 2022.
https://tnc.news/2022/02/03/recap-of-day-12-of-
truckers-for-freedom-convoy-across-
canada%ef%bf%bc/.
Fischer, Sarah. "@GlenMotz Calls out
@Marcomendicino for Attempting to Mislead a
Parliamentary Committee by Spreading Fake News!
#Cdnpoli #EmergenciesAct." Twitter. Twitter, Inc.,
April 26, 2022.
https://twitter.com/SarahFischer__/status/151910
0917446062083.
Forestell, Harry, and David Shipley. "Convoy Protesters
Manipulated by Foreign Agents, Says Cybersecurity
Expert." CBC News. CBC/Radio Canada, 2002.
https://www.cbc.ca/player/play/2002191939918.
Furey, Anthony. "Furey: Liberals Cite CBC 'Analysis' to
Justify Freezing Bank Accounts." Toronto Sun,
February 17, 2022.
https://torontosun.com/opinion/columnists/furey-

liberals-cite-cbc-analysis-to-justify-freezing-bank-accounts.

Golob, Alissa. "After This Elderly Woman Explains to the Police That She Is Participating in the Protest for Her Children and Grandchildren and for 'Peace, Love and Happiness', She Gets Trampled by Policemen on Horseback." Twitter. Twitter, February 18, 2022. https://twitter.com/alissagolob/status/1494815873 944616960.

Gunter, Lorne. "Gunter: More Falsehoods about the Convoy Are Now Being Retracted." ottawasun.com. Postmedia Network Inc., March 12, 2022. https://ottawasun.com/opinion/columnists/gunter-more-falsehoods-about-the-convoy-are-now-being-retracted/wcm/d5dcc94a-5535-4757-b910-8814b10ca508?utm_term=Autofeed&utm_medium =Social&utm_source=Twitter#Echobox=164717058 4.

Hackwill, Robert. "Everything You Always Wanted to Know about Fake News but Were Afraid to Google." euronews, January 24, 2017. https://www.euronews.com/2017/01/24/everythin g-you-always-wanted-to-know-about-fake-news-but-were-afraid-to-google.

Hammer, Alex. "CBC Spreading Conspiracy Theory That 'Russian Actors' Are behind Trucker Vaccine Mandate Protests." Daily Mail Online. Associated Newspapers Ltd, February 2, 2022. https://www.dailymail.co.uk/news/article-10468751/CBC-spreading-conspiracy-theory-Russian-actors-trucker-vaccine-mandate-protests.html.

Information Futures Lab, Claire Wardle, and Stefanie Friedhoff. "Brown School of Public Health Launches

New Lab to Combat Misinformation, Data Deficits, Outdated Communication Practices - and to Catalyze Innovation." Information Futures Lab. Brown School of Public Health - Brown University, June 14, 2022. https://sites.brown.edu/informationfutures/2022/06/14/ifl_launch-2/.

Isidorou, Angelo. "CBC Deletes Story Falsely Claiming Foreign Money behind Freedom Convoy." thepostmillennial.com. The Post Millennial, March 11, 2022. https://thepostmillennial.com/cbc-deletes-story-falsely-claiming-foreign-money-behind-freedom-convoy.

Kolakusic MEP, Mislav. "PM Trudeau, in Recent Months, under Your Quasi-Liberal Boot, Canada Has Become a Symbol of Civil Rights Violations. The Methods We Have Witnessed May Be Liberal to You, but to Many Citizens around the World It Seemed like a Dictatorship of the Worst Kind." Twitter. Twitter, March 23, 2022. https://twitter.com/mislavkolakusic/status/1506702485225938949. Video of the full statement by the Croatian Member of the European Parliament.

Lavoie, Alexandra. "CBC Debunked: The True Story of the Freedom Convoy's 'Victim'." RebelNews.com. Rebel News, March 30, 2022. https://www.rebelnews.com/cbc_debunked_the_true_story_of_the_freedom_convoys_victim.

Lee, Michael. "Free Speech, Freedom Emerging as Top Issues for Canadians: Nanos." CTVNews. CTV News, March 16, 2022. https://www.ctvnews.ca/canada/free-speech-freedom-emerging-as-top-issues-for-canadians-nanos-1.5822003.

Lee, Robert J., ed. "Justin Trudeau Flees to Secret Location." Cairns News, January 31, 2022. https://cairnsnews.org/2022/01/31/justin-trudeau-flees-to-secret-location/.

Lewis, Rebecca, and Alice Marwick. "Media Manipulation and Disinformation Online." Data & Society. Data & Society Research Institute, May 15, 2017. https://datasociety.net/library/media-manipulation-and-disinfo-online/.

Lilley, Brian. "Emergencies Act Regulations Ban Protests except for Indigenous or Refugees." Toronto Sun. Postmedia Network Inc., February 18, 2022. https://torontosun.com/news/national/emergencies-act-regulations-ban-protests-except-for-indigenous-or-refugees.

Ling, Justin. "Was It Really about Vaccine Mandates - or Something Darker? The inside Story of the Convoy Protests." Toronto Star. Toronto Star Newspapers Ltd., March 19, 2022. https://www.thestar.com/news/canada/2022/03/19/was-it-really-about-vaccine-mandates-or-something-darker-the-inside-story-of-the-convoy-protests.html?rf.

Lloyd, Dane. "Ottawa Police Confirm No Firearms Found during Clearing of Convoy Protests." YouTube. Google LLC, March 24, 2022. https://www.youtube.com/watch?v=F_zQe4pCk30.

Lum, Zi-Ann, and Canadian Press. "Top Civil Servant Cautions Politicians of Using 'Words That Lead to Assassination'." HuffPost. The Huffington Post, February 21, 2019. https://www.huffpost.com/archive/ca/entry/michael-wernick-canada-election-violence-assassination_a_23675412.

Malcolm, Candice. "Freeland Caught Holding pro-Nazi Banner at Ukraine Protest." TNC.news. True North Centre for Public Policy, February 28, 2022. https://tnc.news/2022/02/28/freeland-caught-holding-pro-nazi-banner-at-ukraine-protest/.

Malcolm, Candice. "Interference: Freeland's Office 'Pressured' Legacy Media to Change Critical Stories." TNC.news. True North Centre for Public Policy, March 15, 2022. https://tnc.news/2022/03/15/interference-freelands-office-pressured-legacy-media-to-change-critical-stories/.

Malcolm, Candice. "Trudeau, Freeland Met with Ukrainian Neo-Nazi Party Cofounder." TNC.news. True North Centre for Public Policy, March 15, 2022. https://tnc.news/2022/03/15/trudeau-freeland-met-with-ukrainian-neo-nazi-party-cofounder/.

Mangat, Palak. "New: GoFundMe President Juan Benitez Tells #SECU the Company's Review of Where Donations Came from for the Trucker Convoy Fundraising Campaign Showed 88 percent of Donated Funds Originated in Canada, 86 percent of Donors from Canada #Cdnpoli." Twitter. Twitter, March 3, 2022. https://twitter.com/palakmangat/status/14994178 22308540417?s=20&t=n5aaTuD72VtJ4eA1er2juQ.

Marcus, Josh. "Trudeau Moved to Secret Location as Canada Protests Spark Security Fears, Report Says." The Independent. Independent Digital News and Media, January 31, 2022. https://www.independent.co.uk/news/world/ameri cas/justin-trudeau-trucker-convoy-protest-canada-b2003458.html.

McAfee, Dr. Matt. "This Is a Bombshell! Barry Mackilop, a Senior Terrorist Expert for the Gov. of Canada Admits " the Trucker Convoy and It's Supporters Posed No Terrorist Threat, the Only Mistake These People Made Was Believing They Lived in a Free and Democratic Society.'" Twitter. Twitter, March 4, 2022. https://twitter.com/Mattyb59595600/status/14996 76168823484422?s=20&t=l1puwZLo1OrbJmFHZcxh uw.

McKnight, Patricia. "Video Appears to Show Police Horses Trampling Canadian Trucker Protesters." Newsweek. Newsweek Digital LLC, February 22, 2022. https://www.newsweek.com/video-appears-show-police-horses-trampling-canadian-trucker-protesters-1680847.

Media Relations Section. "Man Charged in February Lisgar Street Arson Investigation." Ottawa Police Service. City of Ottawa, March 21, 2022. https://www.ottawapolice.ca/Modules/News/index .aspx?newsId=46eea503-f886-4e7a-9188-edbecabca0a6.

Media Relations Section. "Second Man Charged in February Lisgar Street Arson Investigation." Ottawa Police Service. City of Ottawa, April 6, 2022. https://www.ottawapolice.ca/Modules/News/index .aspx?newsId=46eea503-f886-4e7a-9188-edbecabca0a6.

Murphy, Rex. "Will Anyone Apologize for Falsely Accusing Truckers of Attempted Arson in Ottawa?" National Post. Postmedia Network Inc., April 8, 2022. https://nationalpost.com/opinion/rex-murphy-will-anyone-apologize-for-falsely-accusing-truckers-of-attempted-arson-in-ottawa.

National Post. "Michael Wernick Speaks to Justice Committee." YouTube. Google LLC, February 21, 2019. https://www.youtube.com/watch?v=tXoffOVdd8U.

Orlewicz, Odessa. "Jan 30 - the Sikh Community Fights Back against NDP Leader Jagmeet Singh's Lies & Deception About Convoy." Librti.com. Liberty Talk Canada, January 30, 2022. https://librti.com/page/view-video?id=1675.

Ottawa Police. "We Hear Your Concern for People on the Ground after the Horses Dispersed a Crowd. Anyone Who Fell Got up and Walked Away. We're Unaware of Any Injuries. A Bicycle Was Thrown at the Horse Further down the Line and Caused the Horse to Trip. The Horse Was Uninjured." Twitter. Twitter, February 19, 2022. https://twitter.com/OttawaPolice/status/14950266 64845328388.

Panahi, Rita. "Trudeau Government Has Shown 'Absolutely Totalitarian Behaviour': Douglas Murray." SkyNews.com.au. Nationwide News Pty Ltd, February 22, 2022. https://www.skynews.com.au/opinion/rita-panahi/trudeau-government-has-shown-absolutely-totalitarian-behaviour-douglas-murray/video/8ffe71234e41543ec826730e931b3e88.

Peterson, Dr Jordan B. "Is Justin Trudeau a Coward for Fleeing Canada during Freedom Convoy PROT... Https://T.co/b9ta0z6mnw via @YouTube." Twitter. Twitter Inc., February 6, 2022. https://twitter.com/jordanbpeterson/status/14903 79072630894597.

Pierson, Alex. "Warnings from Former Cabinet Members, Average CRA & We Need New Fuel Rigs." Edited by Tom Korski. Omny.fm. Blacklock's Reporter, March 31, 2022. https://omny.fm/shows/on-point-with-alex-pierson/blacklocks-reporter-check-in-warnings-from-former?t=0s.

Porter, Kate, and Joanne Chianello. "Diane Deans Ousted from Police Services Board by 15 Members of Council | CBC News." CBC News Ottawa. CBC/Radio Canada, February 17, 2022. https://www.cbc.ca/news/canada/ottawa/police-chief-diane-deans-1.6354150.

Postmedia News. "Alleged Arson Attempt Not Connected to Truckers: Ottawa Police." chathamdailynews.ca. Chatham Daily News, a division of Postmedia Network Inc., March 22, 2022. https://www.chathamdailynews.ca/news/provincial/alleged-arson-attempt-not-connected-to-truckers-ottawa-police.

Postmedia News. "CBC Retracts Another Freedom Convoy Story." edmontonsun.com. Edmonton Sun, a division of Postmedia Network Inc., March 11, 2022. https://edmontonsun.com/news/national/cbc-retracts-another-freedom-convoy-story.

Press, Jordan. "MPs Told of Confusion, Panic after Liberals Vowed Financial Crackdown on Convoy." MSN Canada. The Canadian Press, March 17, 2022. https://www.msn.com/en-ca/news/canada/mps-told-of-confusion-panic-after-liberals-vowed-financial-crackdown-on-convoy/ar-AAVcXQQ?ocid=msedgntp.

Press, Jordan. "MPs Told of Confusion, Panic after Liberals Vowed Financial Crackdown on Convoy." MSN News. MSN Canada, March 17, 2022. https://www.msn.com/en-ca/news/canada/mps-told-of-confusion-panic-after-liberals-vowed-financial-crackdown-on-convoy/ar-AAVcXQQ?ocid=msedgntp.

Prestigiacomo, Amanda. "'Tyrant on the Run': Internet Blasts Trudeau for Fleeing Capital as 'Freedom Convoy' Protest Heads His Way." The Daily Wire, January 30, 2022. https://www.dailywire.com/news/tyrant-on-the-run-internet-blasts-trudeau-for-fleeing-capital-as-freedom-convoy-protest-heads-his-way.

Pugliese, David. "Canadian Military Wants to Establish New Organization to Use Propaganda ..." Ottawa Citizen. Postmedia Network Inc., November 2, 2020. https://ottawacitizen.com/news/national/defence-watch/canadian-military-to-establish-new-organization-to-use-propaganda-other-techniques-to-influence-canadians. Pramas, Jason. "The Ottawa Freedom Convoy Occupation: A Local Anarchist Perspective." Digboston.com. Dig Media Group Corporation, February 24, 2022. https://digboston.com/the-ottawa-freedom-convoy-occupation-a-local-anarchist-perspective/.

Raven Dark Media. "Sikh Community Speaks In Ottawa." YouTube. Google LLC, February 18, 2022. https://www.youtube.com/?gl=NL.

Raymond, Ted. "Second Man Charged in Ottawa Arson Case Has No Link to 'Freedom Convoy' Protest: Police." CTV News Ottawa. CTV News, April 6, 2022. https://ottawa.ctvnews.ca/second-man-charged-in-ottawa-arson-case-has-no-link-to-freedom-convoy-protest-police-1.5850922.

Raymond, Ted. "Suspect Charged in Downtown Ottawa Arson Last Month Not Connected with 'Freedom Convoy': Police." CTV News Ottawa. Bell Media, March 21, 2022. https://ottawa.ctvnews.ca/suspect-charged-in-downtown-ottawa-arson-last-month-not-connected-with-freedom-convoy-police-1.5828171.

Rebel News. "Former Congresswoman Tulsi Gabbard, Calls out Trudeau's Handling of the Peaceful Trucker Convoy as: 'Genuinely Authoritarian and Tyrannical' and Refers to Him as the 'Autocratic Leader of Canada.'More: Https://T.co/xgubacy6nq Pic.twitter.com/Qcbwymiapq." Twitter. Twitter, February 27, 2022. https://twitter.com/RebelNewsOnline/status/1498041020423938049?s=20&t=ZeHVKnWt7Rdq8tYlnMN1mw.

Rebel News. "Tulsi Gabbard Calls out Trudeau's Handling of the Trucker Convoy as 'Genuinely Authoritarian and Tyrannical'." Rebel News. Rebel News, February 28, 2022. https://www.rebelnews.com/tulsi_gabbard_calls_out_trudeaus_handling_of_the_trucker_convoy_as_genuinely_authoritarian_and_tyrannical.

Reid, Sheila Gunn. "LEAKED RCMP MESSAGES: 'Time for the Protesters to Hear Our Jackboots on the Ground.'" Rebel News. Rebel News Network Ltd., February 19, 2022. https://www.rebelnews.com/leaked_rcmp_messages_time_for_the_protesters_to_hear_our_jackboots_on_the_ground.

Royal Canadian Mounted Police. "Statement on
 Material Circulating on Social Media Regarding
 Some RCMP Members." Blockades News. Royal
 Canadian Mounted Police, February 20, 2022.
 https://blockade.rcmp.ca/news-nouvelles/ncr-
 rcn201500-s-d-en.html.

Ruhl, Charlotte. "What Is Cognitive Bias?" What Is
 Cognitive Bias? | Simply Psychology. Simply Scholar
 Ltd, May 4, 2021.
 https://www.simplypsychology.org/cognitive-
 bias.html.

Sheikh, Imaan. "OPS Investigating Arson Case after Viral
 Tweets Allege 'Freedom Convoy' Protester
 Involvement." DH News. Buzz Connected Media
 Inc., February 7, 2022.
 https://dailyhive.com/vancouver/ottawa-police-
 arson-investigation-freedom-convoy.

Singh, Jagmeet. "Today We Commemorate 5 Years since
 a Terrorist Attacked and Murdered Muslims in a
 Quebec City Mosque. we said Never Again.and,
 Today Conservative Mps Have Endorsed a Convoy
 Led by Those That Claim the Superiority of the
 White Bloodline and Equate Islam to a Disease."
 Twitter. Twitter Inc., January 29, 2022.
 https://twitter.com/theJagmeetSingh/status/14874
 78167652773888.

Tasker, John Paul. "Thousands Opposed to COVID-19
 Rules Converge on Parliament Hill | CBC News." CBC
 News Politics. CBC/Radio Canada, January 29, 2022.
 https://www.cbc.ca/news/politics/truck-convoy-
 protest-some-key-players-1.6332312.

Tollefson, Jeff. "Tracking QAnon: How Trump Turned
 Conspiracy-Theory Research Upside Down." Nature
 News. Nature Publishing Group, February 4, 2021.

https://www.nature.com/articles/d41586-021-00257-y.

Trudeau, Justin. "Last Night, I Learned That I Have Been Exposed to Covid-19. My Rapid Test Result Was Negative. I Am Following @OttawaHealth Rules and Isolating for Five Days. I Feel Fine and Will Be Working from Home. Stay Safe, Everyone – and Please Get Vaccinated." Twitter. Twitter Inc., January 27, 2022. https://twitter.com/JustinTrudeau/status/1486704 226449379329.

Trudeau, Justin. "Today in the House, Members of Parliament Unanimously Condemned the Antisemitism, Islamophobia, Anti-Black Racism, Homophobia, and Transphobia That We've Seen on Display in Ottawa over the Past Number of Days. Together, Let's Keep Working to Make Canada More Inclusive." Twitter. Twitter Inc., February 1, 2022. https://twitter.com/JustinTrudeau/status/1488660 359422648320.

Unknown. "Canadian Sikhs Have a Message for @JustinTrudeau and @Thejagmeetsingh." Rumble.com, February 19, 2022. https://rumble.com/vvcmay-canadian-sikhs-have-a-message-for-justintrudeau-and-thejagmeetsingh.html.

Unknown. "Trudeau Calls Quebec Woman Racist for Questioning Illegal Immigration." YouTube. Google LLC, August 19, 2018. https://www.youtube.com/?gl=DE.

Urbani, Shaydanay. "Verifying Online Information." First Draft, September 22, 2020. https://firstdraftnews.org/long-form-article/verifying-online-information/.

Van Geyn, Christine, and Joanna Baron. "Opinion: Even after Being Revoked, the Emergencies Act Is Creating a Chill on Charities." nationalpost.com. Postmedia Network Inc., March 8, 2022. https://nationalpost.com/opinion/opinion-even-after-being-revoked-the-emergencies-act-is-creating-a-chill-on-charities.

Vlamis, Kelsey. "Justin Trudeau Was Moved to a Secret Location as Thousands in Canada Protest COVID-19 Vaccine Mandates for Truckers and Other Restrictions." Yahoo! News. Yahoo!, January 29, 2022. https://news.yahoo.com/justin-trudeau-moved-secret-location-014736503.html.

Wakerell-Cruz, Roberto. "Trudeau Liberals' 'Expert Advisory Group on Online Safety' Includes Known Misinformation Spreader Bernie Farber." The Post Millennial. The Post Millennial, March 30, 2022. https://thepostmillennial.com/trudeau-liberals-expert-advisory-group-on-online-safety-includes-known-misinformation-spreader-bernie-farber.

Wardle, Claire, and Carlotta Dotto. "Closed Groups, Messaging Apps and Online Ads." First Draft, September 22, 2020. https://firstdraftnews.org/long-form-article/closed-groups-messaging-apps-and-online-ads/.

Wardle, Claire, and Hossein Derakhshan. "Information Disorder: Toward an Interdisciplinary Framework for Research and Policy Making." Council of Europe. Council of Europe Publishing, September 27, 2017. https://edoc.coe.int/en/media/7495-information-disorder-toward-an-interdisciplinary-framework-for-research-and-policy-making.html.

Wardle, Claire. "Update from First Draft Executive Director Claire Wardle." First Draft, June 14, 2022.

https://firstdraftnews.org/first-draft-update-june2022/.

Wardle, Claire. "10 Questions to Ask before Covering Misinformation." First Draft, 2017. https://firstdraftnews.org/articles/10-questions-newsrooms/.

Wardle, Claire. "5 Lessons for Reporting in an Age of Disinformation." First Draft, December 27, 2018. https://firstdraftnews.org/articles/5-lessons-for-reporting-in-an-age-of-disinformation/.

Wardle, Claire. "Fake News. It's Complicated." First Draft, February 16, 2017. https://firstdraftnews.org/articles/fake-news-complicated/.

Wardle, Claire. "Understanding Information Disorder." First Draft, September 22, 2020. https://firstdraftnews.org/long-form-article/understanding-information-disorder/.

Watt (@tylerwatt90), Tyler. "There Has Been an Increasing Amount of Disturbing Information Related to Possible Foreign Influence of the Trucker Convoy and Illegal Sieges of Cities like Ottawa. Democracy Is Precious and We Must Do Everything to Protect It. I Want to Know Exactly Who Is behind This. #Cdnpoli." Twitter.com, February 11, 2022. https://twitter.com/tylerwatt90/status/149232413 7926287364.

Wittgenstein. "While Discussing His Government's Plan 'to Address Online Harms," Trudeau Says 'We All Have a Responsibility to Deal in Facts and to Fight the Flood of Disinformation and Manipulation." Pic.twitter.com/to75l2KNc." Twitter. Twitter, March 9, 2022. https://twitter.com/backtolife_2022/status/150165

5317100249088?s=20&t=LZ4FkKCLTZNvT44wjbWV1
A.

INDEX

ABOUT THE AUTHORS

Tom Quiggin

Tom is a court expert on jihadist terrorism in the Federal Court of Canada and the Ontario Superior Court. He has testified both for and against followers of the Islamic faith in terrorism cases. He flew as an Airborne Electronic Sensor Operator in CH-124 Helicopters in both the Anti-Submarine Warfare and Search and Rescue roles. He also served as an Intelligence Officer in the Canadian Forces in Bosnia, Croatia, Albania, Russia, and other areas. The RCMP Integrated National Security Enforcement Team (A Div) employed him as a contract intelligence analyst on matters of terrorism and national security for six years. He also was employed in Singapore at Nanyang Technological University on research related to intelligence and national security. Contract work has included the Intelligence Assessment Secretariat of the Privy Council Office of Canada, Citizenship and Immigration Canada and the International War Crimes Tribunal.

Rick Gill

Rick joined the Canadian Forces in 1974. In 1980 after serving in Canada and Europe, Rick transferred to the Canadian Forces' Security Branch and subsequently the newly formed Intelligence Branch in 1982. Rick has served in a variety of domestic and international positions, ranging from the strategic to the tactical, including deployments to Bosnia-Hercegovina, Kosovo, and Afghanistan. In 2009, Rick transferred to the Primary Reserves. At the Canadian Forces School of Military Intelligence, Kingston Ontario, Rick taught analytical methodologies, and served as Sergeant-Major, Standards and Training Development Division. In 2013, Rick retired from the Canadian Forces after 38 years of service and joined Communications Security Establishment Canada, where he co-developed and delivered intelligence analyst training. Rick also volunteered as adjunct faculty with the Privy Council Office's Intelligence Analyst Learning Program, serving Ottawa's Security and Intelligence community. In 2017, Rick joined the Canadian Security Intelligence Service, instructing on analytic training courses; mentoring Service analysts and training development. In 2018, Rick left the Service and now provides consulting services in the Security and Intelligence field.

Manufactured by Amazon.ca
Bolton, ON